"You are a fabulous teacher and gifted ps
Thank you for teaching us your wisdom.
Louise

"I love attending your courses as you have so much knowledge
and you know how to communicate it to others so well."
Phillip

"Thank you for my reading today. I didn't realise how much grief
I had in me. You told me accurate information that no-one else
could have known."
Jessica

"I'll be back for another reading as you are so kind, heartfelt
and attentive. You use your psychic & healing abilities to help
others and for that I am grateful."
Helen

"Your classes are amazing. You stretched us, you got us to tap
into Divine wisdom and you helped us to grow! Thank you
Anna for sharing your passion with us."
Jenni

"You are such a good writer. Your books are easy to follow and
have great exercises in them. Thanks for sharing your insights
and knowledge Anna."
Deb

"You have helped me so much in my life, Anna. Thank you for
guiding me and teaching me to see life in a different way.
You are masterful and brilliant at what you do!"
Alicia

"Life is simple. Everything happens *for* you, not to you. Everything happens at exactly the right moment, neither too soon nor too late. You don't have to like it-it's just easier if you do. If you have a problem, it can only be because of your unquestioned thinking."[1]

1 Byron, K. (2010) *Peace in the Present Moment* (p.72), Hampton Road, VA.

The Spiritual Guidebook

Mastering Psychic Development
and Healing Techniques

By Anna Comerford

ROCKPOOL
PUBLISHING

Published by Rockpool Publishing
PO Box 252
Summer Hill 252, NSW 2130
www.rockpoolpublishing.com.au
www.facebook.com/RockpoolPublishing

First published by Love and Write Publishing in 2017
This edition published by Rockpool Publishing in 2018

National Library of Australia Cataloguing-in-Publication entry:

The spiritual guidebook : mastering psychic development and healing techniques /
Anna Comerford (author).

2nd ed.

9781925682632 (paperback) :

Mind, body, spirit.

Self-help & personal development.

Australian

Edited by Gabiann Marin
Cover design by Farrah Careem
Internal design by Jessica Le, Rockpool Publishing
Typeset by Typeskill
Images by Shutterstock
Printed and bound in China
10 9 8 7 6 5 4 3 2

This book is not intended as a substitute for the medical advice of physicians. The reader
should consult a physician in matters regarding his/her health and particularly with
respect to any symptoms that require diagnosis or medical attention.

PLEASE NOTE: Names have been changed to protect people's privacy.

CONTENTS

Introduction

Thank you for finding this book and calling it into your life. May it take you on a journey to unexpected and magical places for you are a seeker of knowledge and truth.

I have been a perpetual seeker of truth and knowledge my whole life. Spirituality and science has helped me to understand and resolve some challenging situations in my life. In hindsight, I see these situations were to help my soul heal, grow and learn. When we hit rock bottom we can look up and see the light – as there is always a way out. My aim in writing this book is to help others do the same.

This Earth plane is exciting to live on, especially when we delve into the beauty and power of our innate spiritual gifts and divine intelligence. This book helps people to delve deeper into their heart, their soul and the wisdom of the universe. I have seen the powerful changes that psychic and healing knowledge has made in many people's lives, and I hope with the help of the information in this book you too experience positive and profound changes in your own life.

This book is divided into three parts.

Part 1 is about psychic development. This succinct information will help you expand and develop your natural psychic ability, which all humans possess. Chapter 1 covers topics on energy & mind power while Chapter 2 includes information about our psychic senses. Chapter 3 discusses chakras & how to read them while Chapter 4 has interesting information about meditation, visualisation &

self-hypnosis. Chapter 5 shares details about spirits, guides & higher beings while Chapter 6 talks about mediumship, symbols & dreams. Chapter 7 will teach you how to do automatic writing and channelling. Chapter 8 shows you how to read auras & chakras while Chapter 9 describes the art of scrying, psychometry & tea leaf reading.

Part 2 is about the wonders of healing techniques. These chapters cover topics on Reiki, crystal healing, achieving your goals, your health and how to work with clients.

Part 3 mentions amazing facts about our divine universe. There's fascinating information on psychic science, quantum physics and the cosmos. I love when science explains the mystical!

I wish you all the best on your magnificent journey ahead.
May your life flow in ways that surprise and entice you.
May you become the best version of you and keep striving for the love and tranquillity that you deserve.

In Joy,
Anna x

Part 1
Psychic
Development

CHAPTER 1

Energy & Mind Power

You are made of energy that is constantly vibrating. This energy is changeable and transformative. It is amazing how our body, mind and soul has the ability to heal and change. Watching people change, heal and transform has been one of the most humbling and exciting experiences of my life.

The Mind

Most of us have a fast 'monkey mind' that chatters all day in our heads. The trick is to teach this monkey how to slow down and relax. Doing yoga, breathing deeply and meditating can help our mind slow down and be more still. This stillness and centredness helps all areas of our lives as it allows us to tap into our inner self more.

My monkey brain used to be on full alert, but over time I trained my mind to be more grounded by changing routines around food, sleep, exercise and the way I thought. Students, in my courses, really notice the difference with how they think and feel, after doing breathing, meditation and visualisation exercises.

In Figure 1.1 you will notice how slowing down our lovely brain waves, to alpha and theta waves, allows for more intuitive and healing abilities to activate in you.

HUMAN BRAIN WAVES

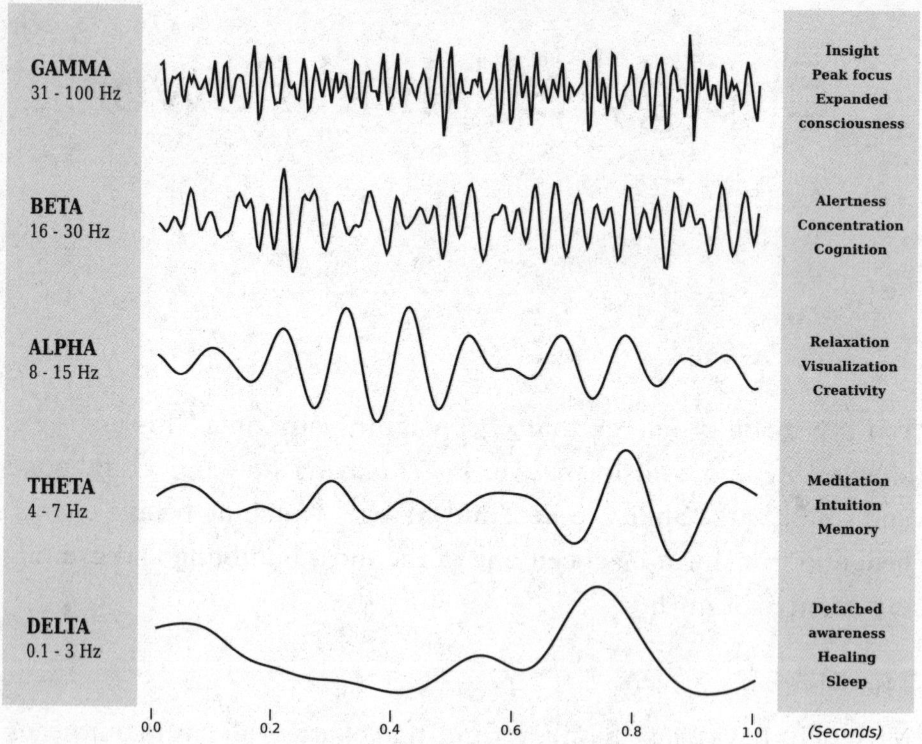

GAMMA 31 - 100 Hz		**Insight** **Peak focus** **Expanded** **consciousness**
BETA 16 - 30 Hz		**Alertness** **Concentration** **Cognition**
ALPHA 8 - 15 Hz		**Relaxation** **Visualization** **Creativity**
THETA 4 - 7 Hz		**Meditation** **Intuition** **Memory**
DELTA 0.1 - 3 Hz		**Detached** **awareness** **Healing** **Sleep**

0.0   0.2   0.4   0.6   0.8   1.0   (Seconds)

Figure 1.1 Human Brain Waves

You've probably heard of the terms conscious and subconscious mind. The conscious mind includes our short-term memory as well as our ability to plan and think critically. The subconscious mind includes our long-term memories and emotions. The subconscious mind also contains our habits, patterns and creativity. The superconscious mind is universal wisdom and power.

How powerful is your subconscious mind?

Can you believe that the subconscious mind is a million times more powerful than our conscious mind![2] My clients are very surprised when I tell them how powerful our subconscious is. Our thoughts and feelings are an important way to tap into the subconscious mind as it works well with images and emotions/feelings. Visualisations and meditations are effective as they imprint information into our subconscious, which helps to break patterns and beliefs that we don't need.

The superconscious mind goes beyond our consciousness, into a realm of all-knowing, all-being where wisdom and insight exist. When we go into deeper states of being, we can tap into this vast warehouse of data to find out what makes us tick.

Why do we need to breathe deeply?

I invite you, while you are reading this book, to be aware of your breathing. Are you breathing from your abdomen or lungs? Good breathing is when the abdomen rises first, then your lungs rise afterwards.

Try breathing ten deep slow belly breaths. Notice how you drop into a slower alpha/theta brain wave state. Many clients come to a session in a beta brain wave state. After deep breathing they enter into a deeper alpha/theta state that allows for more healing, intuition and relaxation to occur.

BRAIN WAVES

Table 1.1

| GAMMA | Gamma waves are important for learning, memory and information processing. It is believed gamma waves tap into our superconscious. |
| BETA | Beta waves include our conscious thought and logical thinking. We are in beta when we read, write and socialise with others. Beta waves are good for memory and problem solving. |

---

2 Lipton, B. (2013) *Honeymoon Effect*, (p.75) Hay House, USA

ALPHA	Alpha waves link between our conscious thinking and subconscious mind. Meditation and yoga can help put us into an alpha state.
THETA	Theta waves occur when we're sleeping or daydreaming. Theta is a deeply relaxed state. Helps us tap into the subconscious and beyond.
DELTA	Delta waves are our slowest recorded brain waves. Delta waves affect unconscious areas such as heartbeat and digestion. Delta waves include our dreams, astral travel and deep healing. Links us to the superconscious.

Question: How many thoughts do we have per minute?

Answer: Most people have 48.6 thoughts every minute![3] That's nearly one thought per second! This equals about 70,000 thoughts per day which is a lot of words and energy in our heads on a daily basis.

How are you using this energy?

Are you like a parrot repeating the same negative or depressing thoughts each day or, are you kind to yourself and put up a filter which deciphers what thoughts and images are allowed into your mind? What percentage of your thoughts are negative, or positive? Do you speak to yourself with love or admonish and berate yourself? If you find yourself falling more into the negative thoughts, consider how that is making you feel. Would a young child benefit from being put down and chastised all the time? Of course not!

Don't get me wrong, compassionate constructive criticism is healthy, the key is to determine the purpose and tone of the thoughts, are they constructive or destructive? Internal emotional thoughts can be your haven but only if you are gentle on yourself when you make mistakes, laugh it off and try again. We are on this earth plane to practise, redo and be triumphant.

---

3 https://www.google.com.au/search?q=uni+of+southern+california+research+thoughts+per+min&

Exercise: Word Power

Think to yourself right now, "I am alive". When you think these words, in your mind, where are they coming from? You have a voice that you hear inside your head when you speak to yourself, for example say in your mind "I need some water". You may find those words come from the middle of your head area. You may experience something different so take note of that.

Keep saying sentences silently to yourself and hear the vibrations of those words in your body. Close your eyes and say internally "I am awful" repeat internally several times. What do you feel? What do you notice happens in your body? Now repeat "I am joy" internally several times. How do you feel? What happens in your body? Once you are tuned into your own inner voice then you can tune into the subtle vibrations of Spirit messages and you can notice the difference in Spirit language to your own inner voice.

Psychic Abilities

I believe that we are all have psychic and intuitive abilities. Even though we were born with two physical eyes, we are also gifted with a third eye. This third eye lives, energetically, between our eyebrows and is linked to our pineal gland. By doing certain exercises, your third eye will become more open and expanded so you will be able to 'see' more images and visions.

We have so much power within us to activate and heal ourselves. Knowledge can help us find this inner power. It's time to get it on!

Joe's Visions

One day Joe arrived at my clinic. Joe said he was more auditory than visual as he had a good ear for music. Joe said he couldn't see spirits or have visions. He wanted to open up his third eye so

I asked Joe to imagine a green apple. Then I asked him to tell me whether this green apple was in his mind's eye or floating around somewhere just in front of his face. I then asked him to imagine that he was looking at a big movie screen.

He imagined he was sitting in a movie theatre looking at a large screen (magic screen) in front of him. I now suggested that Joe imagine that his car was up on this screen. I asked him to hop in his car and watch himself driving it away. Joe saw that image quite well. The next task was for Joe to imagine himself opening the front door of his house and walking through it. Joe agreed he could imagine that as well. He was surprised that he could visualise so easily! Visualising and seeing in our minds eye is a skill we all have we just have to practise so the third eye is strengthened, but if it's hard for you to access start by visualising things you are familiar with which will open up your visualisation skills.

Magic Screen

The Magic Screen represents the view your third eye has. Remember the more you use your Magic Screen the more your third eye ability will grow and expand and the more clairvoyant you can become!

Talk to your body

William said his left thigh was sore. I asked William "if the pain could speak what would it say?" He replied "I'm angry!" I asked William to allow an image to come to him. He closed his eyes and breathed and allowed any insights from his higher self to come through. William recalled that at age 5 he had been very angry with his brother and that no-one supported him. We discussed how this pent-up anger was affecting him now and, how he could support himself when strong emotions like anger came up for him to face, resolve and heal.

Tips to Heal Self:

1. Go to a natural environment so the earth can help to heal you. (Or imagine the room you are in is a gorgeous rainforest). Gently move your body so your chakras can activate. Walk, breathe deeply, do yoga or stretch. Your body is designed to move. Moving your body allows your organs, aura and chakras to be revitalised and cleansed. This will activate deep healing.

2. Ask for guidance and open your senses to receive Divine information. If you have an issue/concern, ask for answers about what is happening.

3. Close your eyes and tap into your inner knowingness.

4. Ask your body and soul to share with you how it's feeling. For example, if you have a sore hip ask your hip what emotions it feels. You may get an answer back as a colour, image or feeling.

5. Put golden white light healing around self.

6. Continue to drink water and herbal teas. Put high vibration and healing foods into your body such as nuts, fruit and vegetables as these will help to activate the healing response in your body and your cells will love you filling your body with these powerful foods.

The Activation exercise below is great to do regularly. One of my clients said she didn't need her morning coffee after doing this exercise as it boosted her energy so much!

Exercise: Anna's 4 Step Activation Sequence:

This exercise is very grounding and prepares the mind, body and soul for heightened intuition and more joy into your being. The

Activation exercise is great to do regularly and it helps prepare me for a day of clients.

Put on relaxing music if you wish.

1. **Rainbow Cleanse:** Imagine breathing rainbow colours into your body and out into the space around you. This will cleanse your energy field.

2. **Beam of Light:** Imagine a glowing, golden white pillar of light beaming down from the sky above you. Move this light down through your body, like a shining beam of light until it reaches down into the earth below you. Imagine this beam of light goes into the centre of the earth then, imagine it returning back up through your body again and flows out through the top of your head. Continue bringing this pillar of light down into the earth again and up again to the crown chakra. Allow this cycle to continue several times.

   This powerful light beam will create a vortex of healing, grounding and rejuvenating light which will enlarge and enhance your aura and energy field. Feel the expansion around you.

3. **Trance:** Close your eyes and take several big belly breaths and slowly breathe in and out. Relax your shoulders and body.

   a) Breathe in for 4 seconds

   b) Hold your breath for 4 seconds

   c) Now breathe out 4 seconds

   d) Hold your breath for 4 seconds – then repeat the cycle again.

   Continue this relaxing breathing cycle. Do this 5–10 times so your alpha/theta brain waves are activated. Have the intention that all your chakras are opening up in a healthy way for you. Feel deeply relaxed as you continue this slow breathing, in and out.

   Note: Ten of these deep belly breath cycles will take you into a relaxing alpha/theta trance-like state.

4. **Ask:** Now ask for your spirit guide/higher self to assist you clearly and effectively. Call them in three times as this is known to be more powerful. It's like ringing up the spirit hotline to help you. They need three requests from us so they can connect better with your energy field and vibration.

Now that you are tuned in, open up your "clairs" (see Chapter 2) and connect to what you feel, sense, see, know, taste and smell around you.

Note: I like to imagine I'm in a rainforest or am surrounded by large crystals of energy, as this helps me to tune into my clairs better. Other times I imagine each chakra has a crystal in it protecting it and giving it healing energy. Do what is best for you.

Psychic Senses & Seven Levels

Seven Psychic Clairs

'Clair' is a French word meaning 'clear' and we refer to the way in which we access spiritual messages through a number of different senses as the clairs. You may of heard of the term Clairvoyance, but there are several other ways messages can be received from the spirit realm.

The seven main psychic clairs are:

1. Clairsentience (clear feeling and sensing, may be called clairempathy)
2. Clairvoyance (clear seeing or vision)
3. Clairaudience (clear hearing)
4. Clairtangency (clear touching, may be known as psychometry)
5. Claircognizance (clear knowing)
6. Clairgustance (clear tasting)
7. Clairalience (clear smelling, sometimes called clairscent)

Clairsentience

Clairsentience is often the first and easiest to develop as it's linked to gut feelings and hunches. This psychic feeling and sensing is linked to emotions and feelings. You may be able to sense if someone is sad or is not telling the truth. Our nervous system is electrical so it has a psychic antenna that picks up different waves and vibrations of energy.

Clairvoyance

Clairvoyant people may have prophetic visions or dreams of the future. This is called a premonition.

You may experience clairvoyance by having dreams, visions, mental images or movies that appear in your mind or third eye area. Other signs of clairvoyance include seeing colours (auras) around people, plants and animals; having a good sense of direction and easily visualising solutions to problems. Clairvoyant people are good with visual-spatial problems and may like rearranging furniture!

Clairaudience

This is the ability to hear messages through our auditory systems. People who play instruments, sing or write songs are usually auditory so they may be good at clairaudience. The messages themselves don't have to be actual sounds, that is just how the clairaudient perceives them. Sometimes a clairaudient person may pick up on thoughts of people around them (called mental telepathy). If a spirit is communicating with you, it may feel like it comes from outside your head and may be in a slightly different octave to the vibration of your own thoughts. Sometimes I hear specific words being said, while other times it's more like an energetic or telepathic type vibration that I 'hear'.

Feet

I was getting ready for a client recently when I called in my guide. I heard "sore feet" which puzzled me. I had just been gardening but my feet were OK. I finished getting ready and sat in front of my client Jade. I asked Jade how her day had been.

"My feet are aching, I've been on my feet all day in high heels!" The universe is wise and all knowing. Tap into that superconscious energy. It's so full of love for us.

Clairtangency

Clairtangency is also called psychometry. This is another form of clairsentience. Psychometry is when you gain information from touching an object, person or animal. You may also get intuitive vibes from a hug, a handshake, brushing up against someone or sitting in someone's chair. You may also get psychic impressions when you are holding someone's jewellery, article of clothing or a letter.

Claircognizance

Claircognizance is a strong sense of knowing. It's when you get wisdom and information, in the form of ideas and concepts, that suddenly come to you. This knowingness seems to come from somewhere other than your own thoughts, although it can seem closely linked. Claircognizance is when you just seem to know something. It might feel odd but it's usually accurate. I once did a psychic reading for a client named Liz. I connected with Liz's mum who had passed away many years prior. Throughout the reading I had this unusual knowingness that Liz felt responsible for her mother's death. I shared this claircognisant information with Liz who burst into tears and told me she did indeed feel guilty around the circumstances of her mother's death. By having that extra knowledge in the reading I was able to help Liz process her guilt and let go of the trauma around the incident and to know that her mother had crossed over in peace.

Clairgustance and Clairalience

These two psychic abilities are not common. Clairgustance is when you taste something yet there's nothing in your mouth. Clairalience is smelling something when that smell is not around you! Some people may smell a perfume scent when they are doing mediumship. This perfume may be linked to a woman in spirit who is coming through to pass on a specific message. Some people taste meat in their mouth if the person they are reading for needs to eat meat or may be low in iron.

Onion Message

I was cooking in the kitchen and had put all the ingredients into the pan. The word "onion" floated down into my mind. I knew the word "onion" didn't come from my mind. I had forgotten to put onions in my recipe and my Guide gently popped the word "onion" into my mind! The word onion was so quiet and subtle that I could have thought it was from my own mind. This story is simple but it's an example of how the universe supports us. Be aware of those subtle messages that float into your mind and consciousness.

Seven Levels

It is believed that there are seven levels of existence.

Level 1: Minerals, mountains and earth

Level 2: Trees, plants, herbs, flowers

Level 3: Humans and animals live on this 3rd plane. Here we learn to manifest, to be aware of our actions, thoughts and deeds so we can create more harmony and success in our lives.

Level 4: On this level are the spirits that have crossed over such as relatives and animals. Some people can see or feel spirits on this level. They may appear as shadows, colours or vibrations.

Level 5: This level consists of Higher Beings of Light and Spirit guides who support us on the earth plane. Crystal energies are also on this plane as well as unicorns and some other animals.

Level 6: The Blueprint of All that is, containing as the Akashic records and Past lives. Holds the Divine Plan for the Universe.

Level 7: All THAT IS, Oneness of Life, Eternal Joy, LOVE.

Note: All levels intertwine and merge with each other.

Exercise: Call in Higher Energies

You can call on the energy and power of the Levels to support and Guide you. Remember to ask for energies that Love You Unconditionally. Ask 3 times so you know that you will attract the right energies to you. It's like dialling a phone number but instead you say this invocation/request.

Invocation

"I call in Divine energies which love me unconditionally. All other energies can go to the Light where there is love & healing waiting for you."

Repeat three times.

If I am with a client and I need more energy and support I will say this in my mind and the energy in the room will shift. It's a powerful, simple process to do.

CHAPTER 3

Chakras & How to Read Them

People are always keen to know more about chakras and how they influence and impact our feelings, actions and thoughts. They are indeed very powerful and you can tap into the energy of the chakras to reveal information about yourself or people you are working with.

Chakra is a Sanskrit term which means wheel of light.[4] There are seven main chakras that exist in our body. Each chakra helps access and deliver certain forms of energy into our body. They also give energy to organs, nerves, muscles and bones. Chakras are like musical notes because they vibrate at different frequencies. The more you know about them the more skilled you will be at tuning into the human body.

Chakras allow energy to flow in and out of our body and are just as vital and important as our bodily organs. They are linked to our body via glands and nerves.

---

4 Dale, C. (2010) *The Complete Book of Chakra Healing*, Llewellyn, Minnesota.

They are also known as wheels of energy that spin in a clockwise or anticlockwise direction. Each chakra has a different vibration, just like different chords on a guitar make a different sound. If we live an unhealthy lifestyle the chakra wheels can become out of tune and as a result our physical body can suffer.

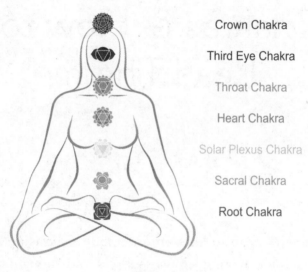

Crown Chakra

Third Eye Chakra

Throat Chakra

Heart Chakra

Solar Plexus Chakra

Sacral Chakra

Root Chakra

Figure 3.1

Chakras are like a vortex of energy that are constantly moving and changing depending on our thoughts, actions and foods we eat.

Chakras hold energy and can store information. They can get blocked especially if we do not move our body and process our emotions. Our lungs, for example, hold the energy of grief. If this grief is not released we may get chest pains or asthma because the chakra wheel will not turn as efficiently due to these blocked emotions. My friend Ann gets asthma if blocked emotions get stored in her chest. After Ann has a good cry her breathing becomes easier and she feels better.

Emotions are good to have as they communicate to us what our body is feeling. Emotions are meant to move through us, so that we learn to love, heal, forgive and be more at peace in life.

Our Chakras

You will find that websites and books will share different meanings and explanations of the chakras. I mostly refer to the 12 Chakra System. See the table below for a summary of these 12 chakras.[5]

Table 3.1

CHAKRA	Colour	Gland (Endocrine / Hormonal)	Location
1. Root/Base	Red	Adrenals	Hip / Genitals
2. Sacral	Orange	Ovaries / Testes	Abdomen
3. Solar Plexus	Yellow	Pancreas	Solar plexus
4. Heart	Green, pink, gold	Heart	Heart
5. Throat	Blue	Thyroid	Throat
6. Third eye	Purple, indigo	Pituitary	Forehead
7. Crown	White, clear, violet	Pineal	Crown
8. Records (Past lives, Akashic)	Silver, ultraviolet black	Thymus	4cm above head
9. Soul	Gold or infra-red	Diaphragm	Arm's length above head
10. Grounding	Brown, yellows, greens	Bones	30–100cm below feet
11. Transmute	Pink	Connective tissue & meridians	Palms and soles of feet
12. Purpose	No colour as these are points on body	32 points	Points around the body

The Akashic records are known as the book of life. This is where all information of all our past, and current lifetimes, are recorded. Akashic records are shown in the 8th chakra near the head area.

The 9th chakra is about your Soul's essence. It's a powerful and beautiful chakra – a doorway where we can receive Divine

5 Dale, C. (2010) *The Complete Book of Chakra Healing*, Llewellyn, Minnesota.

information and have communication and connection with Higher Beings and Guides. The 9th chakra is linked to the moon's energies.

Remember we have free will and the Guides know we have to walk our own path and make our own conscious decisions. It is for our highest good, and the benefit of others, if we make decisions based on love, integrity and with good intention. The Guide's job is to support and look out for us. They may send us signs such as a song, words or a dream.

Cleansing with the Chakras

The 11th Chakra is found in the hands and feet. It's where we can absorb energy from around us. It's also a good place to release pent-up energy by putting our hands towards the earth and asking for any excess energy to be released. Taking your shoes off and placing the soles of your feet on the natural ground is also an excellent way of cleansing your aura and energy field and recharging yourself.

Crystal Cave

Belinda arrived for her Reiki healing session. She was concerned about her health and the intimacy with her partner. Belinda relaxed on the massage table while I placed a blanket over her body. As I was completing the Reiki healing I was guided to do a visualisation with Belinda. She imagined going into a magical cave full of huge powerful crystals.

A guide showed me that Belinda was a nun in a previous lifetime. I told Belinda that her feminine side was currently being challenged by some old beliefs from that lifetime. I could feel lots of powerful energy coming through my hands from the Reiki energy. Belinda cried as the shifts in her mind, body and soul were gently taking place.

We could both feel the huge release and healing that was happening. I clairvoyantly saw the Guides work on her solar plexus chakra and other chakras. Afterwards Belinda revealed that in this lifetime her mother wanted her to be a nun!

After our healing session Belinda's relationship with her health, and her partner, improved dramatically.

Exercise: Chakra Meditation

Steps for your chakra meditation are:

1. Start your chakra meditation by sitting in a comfortable position with your spine straight, but not rigid. You may lie down if you wish to. If the mind wanders (which it is designed to do) just gently bring it back and keep focusing on your breathing, your stillness and your calmness.

2. Now focus on each part of your body. Begin with your feet and work up towards your head. As you do this, tell that part of your body to relax and let the stress melt away.

   Start at your feet. Say to yourself words similar to this: "I am aware of my feet, I breathe energy down to my feet. As I breathe in and out I feel more and more relaxed."

   Next say: "I am aware of my legs, I breathe energy into my legs and as I breathe in and out I feel more and more relaxed." Continue on doing your torso, arms, neck then head.

3. Imagine the space around you is filled with rainbow colours. Breathe those rainbow colours into your body as you relax deeper and deeper.

4. Now we give extra energy to each chakra.

   Start with the base chakra and work your way up to the crown chakra.

Imagine a red colour in the 1st base chakra and visualise this vibrant red colour emanating in the whole room around you.

Imagine an orange colour in the sacral 2nd chakra and visualise this vibrant orange colour emanating in the whole room around you.

Imagine a yellow colour in the solar plexus 3rd chakra and visualise this vibrant yellow colour emanating in the whole room around you.

Imagine a pink colour in the heart 4th chakra and visualise this serene pink colour emanating in the whole room around you.

Imagine a blue colour in the throat 5th chakra and visualise this luminous blue colour emanating in the whole room around you.

Imagine a purple/indigo colour in the third eye 6th chakra and visualise this majestic purple, indigo colour emanating in the whole room around you.

Imagine a violet/white colour in the crown 7th chakra and visualise this brilliant violet/white colour emanating in the whole room around you.

Imagine a silver colour in the records 8th chakra and visualise this shining silver colour emanating in the whole room around you.

Imagine a gold colour in the soul 9th chakra and visualise this glowing gold colour emanating in the whole room around you.

Imagine brown/green colours in the 10th grounding chakra and visualise these earthy brown/green colours emanating in the whole room around you.

Imagine a deep pink colour in the palms and feet, of the 11th chakra, and visualise this deep pink colour emanating in the whole room around you.

5. Breathe in energies from the cosmos. Relax and breathe deeply and slowly. Allow this energy to encompass your entire body and infuse your aura with divine energy. Visualise this incredible energy making your aura stronger, brighter and more resilient.

Sacral Relationship

Stephanie came to see me for a healing because she was suffering from bladder infections. Bladder infections metaphysically may mean a person is "pissed off" about something. I asked, in my mind, to view her chakras.

I saw a colour around her sacral chakra and I also saw a male image in there. I was also shown the letter B. I asked Stephanie, was there a male starting with the letter B significant to her? Stephanie started to cry as she confirmed that Brendan was her ex-husband. She was really annoyed with Brendan as they were having issues with their co-parenting arrangement. I saw a dark-coloured cord extending from her abdomen (3rd chakra) to Brendan. (When we are corded in a healthy way the cord is a lighter colour).

I took Stephanie through a healing meditation and visualisation where she was happy to let go of past hurts, forgive him and wish him well. We did a healing and released Brendan with love. She contacted me the next day to say that her bladder irritation had gone and that she was feeling emotionally and mentally better!

These types of healings are powerful not only for the client but for their children and families as the healing energetically affects everyone around us.

According to research the way the parents relate in a home affects the children's immune systems. The research[6] also states that when partners are sarcastic to each other they not only diminish the couple's happiness but, also their immune systems and health. The partner, and children, who are hearing the sarcasm will have more infectious illnesses in the following year! So remember that your energy, thoughts and emotions have a powerful effect on others.

6 Gottman J. & Gottman J. (2015) *Doing effective couples therapy* (p.19) Norton, NY.

Note: Not everyone is able to forgive and let go all in the one session. It may take a while for some people to move through their emotions depending on the circumstances. It's best for clients to travel at their own pace. Guide them gently.

"To forgive means to let go of our negative feelings like resentment, judgement, condemnation, anger, and the desire to 'get even', to see someone punished or hurt. It frees you from unpleasant feelings and victim mentality. Such feelings make people live in the past, feel unhappy and creates tension and disease in their body."[7]

How to Read Chakras

Preparation:

To tune into a chakra it's best to meditate first to heighten your intuitive energies. Do the exercise titled **Chakra Meditation** as this will enhance your intuitive abilities and psychic awareness.

Ask, in your mind, for the chakras to reveal themselves to you. You may see all of them open up but usually it's one or two. This is good as it will usually be the chakra that needs the most attention and focus in the session. You may find the chakra will reveal a colour, an image or a feeling to you.

Connect and merge with that chakra. The more you tune into it the more it will reveal to you. Breathe and relax and trust the information that comes through to you. Open up your psychic clairs and ask for more information so you can gain more clarity. One day a client's sacral chakra showed an image of stitches around her abdominal area. I asked the superconscious for more information and I felt that she was still healing in this area. The client revealed that she was recovering from a hysterectomy.

---

7 Orr, L. & Van Laere, F. (2011) *Manual for Rebirthers* (p.112), Aadimaya, India.

Exercise: Read Your Own Chakras:

Close your eyes and go within (or visualise yourself in a white bubble of light). Ask a chakra to connect with you and sense the colours, images, sounds, feelings that come to you. What does that area and body are want to say to you?

Exercise: Read Other's Chakras:

Ask friends or family members if you can tune into their chakras. Ask them questions so you can practise. This will help you learn about how to tune into your psychic senses more.

Also, look at animals and see what their chakras reveal to you. Remember that the chakras are dynamic energy that are always changing and evolving. The chakras want to share information with you so go ahead and converse with these magnificent chakras.

Sounds

As you know sounds are vibrations. When you sing, or let out a growl, it makes you feel different as the vibrations are vibrating through-out your whole body and aura. Sound vibrations move like a wave throughout your body and aura. Energy (emotions) move around and make way for new energy to come into our chakras and cells.

The emotion of sadness, for example, may move out of your heart chakra and may travel up your body as you feel the energy of sadness. Tears may even flow as this emotion travels through your body. Anger stuck in one of your chakras may be released via shouting or with fast breathing.

Singing melodies can help to harmonise the chakras. Being silent can also be powerful to rest your chakras and help them recharge. Chanting repetitive mantras helps the chakras realign as well.

Each chakra is linked to an octave note. That's why when we listen to music and sounds it makes us feel certain emotions. Music has a direct effect on our chakras and energy centres. I like to put on calming music when I am busily typing on my computer. Soothing music can help keep us calm and focused. When my daughter was young I would put peaceful music on in the mornings so that we would both get ready for the day in a more cohesive, gentle way.

Table 3.2

Chakra/Aura Level	Octave Note
1	C
2	D
3	E
4	F
5	G
6	A
7	B

"Your voice is a built-in sound-healing tool."[8]

Exercise: Sound Healing

1. Close your eyes and begin to hum. Notice what part of your body the humming comes from. How does it make you feel?

2. Mantra: Chant a repetitive sound or word. You can say these words silently to yourself or out loud. For example:

   "I am peace"

   "I am calm"

   "I am love"

   or "Joy … Joy … Joy … Joy …"

   Notice how the energy of these words make you feel.

---

8 Dale, C. (2013) *The Subtle Body Practise manual*, (p.295) Sounds True, US.

Exercise: Chakra Sounds

Sounds are a good way to help activate and re-energise the chakras.

The sound of the Sacral chakra is **Ooh**

The sound of the Heart chakra is **Ah**

The sound of the Crown chakra is **Eee**

Close your eyes, if you wish and allow the sounds to emanate through you.

Begin by doing one sound at a time to fully embrace the vibration of each sound.

Begin with repeating the **Ooh** sound and feel where the sound vibrates in your body.

Now say **Ah** and feel where this sounds permeates in your body and aura.

Now say **Eee** and feel where this sounds ripples in your body and aura.

Now let's merge the sounds slowly together. Flow the three sound together:

Ooh ... Ah ... Eee.

Repeat several times. Tune into the energy of the three sounds combined.

How do you feel after doing this?

CHAPTER 4

Meditation, Visualisation & Self-Hypnosis

It's easy to get caught up in technology such as mobiles, computers and television. The lure of the screen keeps us trapped and enticed. We get entranced by information, pictures and constant stimulation. Even though technology is useful in moderate doses, its constant whirlwind of colour and stimulus can lock us in the mind and keep us stuck in the left logical brain.

The right brain needs time to expand and grow so our intuition, gut feeling, can be activated. There's a tranquil internal world awaiting us. Even though our inner world may seem so still and sedate, it brings us centeredness and a quietness which allows that inner voice to be heard and, most importantly, our inner eye to have vision.

Meditation allows the windows of the soul to open and lets more celestial light into one's body. Yoga and movement, even walking, is like a moving meditation that increases energy, awareness and peace in the body, mind and soul.

My meditation practise over the years has been on and off. There were times when I did meditation regularly and other times I stayed on the hamster wheel of life. Over time I've become more consistent with meditation as I began to fall in love with the wonderful benefits it gave to me. Before I see clients, I jump on my mini-trampoline, do a few gentle yoga stretches and meditate. While meditating I call in my guides and ask Spirit to help me. This ritual helps my heart to open and my chakras expand. I feel the energy increase in my aura as the Chi (life force energy) flows into my cells.

Benefits of Meditation

Meditation is beneficial in so many areas of our lives. Meditation is great for reducing depression, improves the immune system and helps us focus.[9] Meditation reduces pain and inflammation. It also helps with self-control and creates positive emotions.

Scientists discovered that people who learned meditation have a thickening in their brain. The areas in which the brain actually thickened were in the areas of **learning, thinking and memory**.

Meditation also helps with emotional balance as well as empathy and compassion. The brain stem (where neurotransmitters are made to pass on information) is enhanced as well. Meditation reduces stress levels as the amygdala, fight or flight area of our brain, becomes calmer.

Meditations for You

The meditations below will help you to centre and focus. I have used the exercises in courses and with clients. Your body and brain changes after regular meditation. It relaxes, slows down to a different rhythm and it connects you in a way that enhances everything in your life.

---

9 https://www.psychologytoday.com/blog/feeling-it/201309/20-scientific-reasons-start-meditating-today

Exercise: Wish upon a Star Meditation

1. Bring awareness to your heart and belly.

2. Breathe deeply several times in and out.

3. Ask yourself: How am I feeling in this moment? Honour your thoughts and feelings. To feel is to heal.

   Why are you feeling those feelings? Let them have a voice.

   Write down your feelings or, talk to a counsellor if you need assistance to sort out your feelings.

4. Wish upon A Star. Ask yourself: What do you wish for in life?

   Imagine what your wishes would look like if they became real. See those images in your mind or, imagine them up on a big movie screen where you are the main actor. Play the movie and see your aims and goals being acted out by you!

   Feel the emotions, the joy, the happiness of achieving your dreams and wishes. Put colour and sound to your images so your subconscious sees them as real. Your subconscious doesn't know the difference between fact or fantasy so your thoughts are reality to your subconscious.

Trust

Trust is a value that may take time to develop. Can you trust that what comes to you in life is the best outcome for your highest self? Or, do you think what comes along your path is bad, wrong and disappointing?

What if that event that upset you was actually needed to help you be more humble and compassionate? Would you give lollies to a young child in a grocery store simply because they wanted the lollies, or would you teach them to wait and learn self-control? Well the same is true with the events in our lives. The Universe won't give us all the sweets at once. It waits until we are ready and teaches us how to moderate our wants and desires, so that we can gain the best outcome and, not get a belly ache from too much junk food!

Sometimes we learn from the challenging paths we walk down. Our soul may need those paths to bring to us the learning and gifts we need at that point in time. Some of the hardest challenges in my life have been the most rewarding opportunities for me. Initially I may not have thought this but, as time went on I realised these circumstances paved the way for the next adventure to occur.

We need to have healthy boundaries so we can grow and develop in a way that is right for our Soul. Spirit knows what we need and how to help shape us into Beings of Light that are loving, compassionate and respectful to self and others.

Exercise: Trampoline **Dome** (TD) Meditation

TD Breathing is when you use your diaphragm to breath deep nurturing breaths. The **diaphragm** is a dome shaped muscle under your ribs and is the main muscle used in effective breathing.

The **diaphragm** divides the abdominal area from the upper part of our body. "It is a dome-shaped sheet of muscle that is inserted into the lower ribs."[10]

You know you are using your diaphragm effectively when:

a) your belly fills with air first then,

b) your lungs fill up with air next.

c) thirdly your shoulders may rise up a little too.

d) when you exhale pay attention to your breath leaving your body. Notice how relaxed you feel as you breathe out and let go.

---

10 www.healthline.com

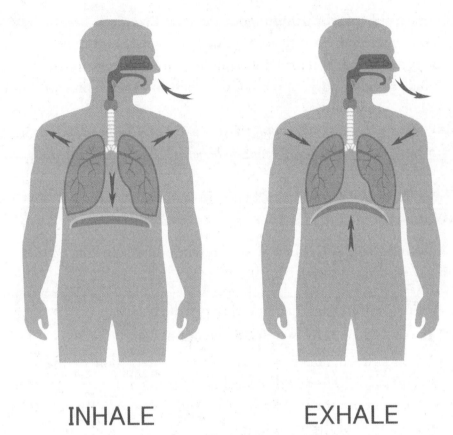

INHALE   EXHALE

Figure 4.1

To begin TD breathing:

1. Inhale (through your nose if possible) then exhale out your mouth.

2. Feel the gentle rising and falling of your abdomen.

    Feel your diaphragm/dome (under your ribs) rise and fall like a trampoline mat. Place your hand above your belly button to feel your body move up and down as your breath flows in and out of your body.

3. Inhale and exhale again. Breathe slower and deeper. Feel your lungs expand in your chest as you take in the (chi) energy from the air around you. Repeat slowly several times.

4. Repeat this practice throughout the day. Take deep breaths regularly to remind yourself to breathe consciously and to relax your body and mind. You may notice an increase in energy in your head, hands or other parts of the body as the Chi energy enhances your energy and vitality.

When you practise TD regularly you will begin to breathe that way unconsciously and you'll reap the benefits!

Exercise: Mantra Word Meditation

A Mantra is:

"a sound, word, or phrase that is **repeated** by someone who is praying or meditating."[11]

1. Begin by sitting, or lying, in a comfortable position.
2. Take slow, deep belly breaths in and out of your body.
3. Choose a word that makes you feel relaxed, such as the word Loving, Relax, Calming or Peaceful.

   If we choose the word relax we would breathe in the word RE and breathe out the word LAX.

   Re-lax : Breathe in RE Breathe out LAX.

   As you take slow deep breaths in and out repeat the word in your mind. Continue to repeat the word (mantra) over in your mind as you gently breathe in and out. Feel your body relax and your mind become centred. When thoughts come into your mind simply notice them and let them float way like a moving cloud. Return to your mantra. Choose a different word, if you wish, such as:

   Calm-ing: Breathe in CALM Breathe out ING

   Lov-ing: Breathe in LOV Breathe out ING

   Peace-ful: Breathe in PEACE Breathe out FUL

---

11 http://www.merriam-webster.com/dictionary/mantra

Exercise: Walking In Love (W.I.L) Meditation

1. Find a place to walk. Choose a place inside or outside in nature. Walk very slowly and feel relaxed as you place one foot in front of the other. Breathe deeply in and out of your belly several times.

2. When thoughts come into your mind simply notice them and let them float away like a moving cloud.

3. As you walk be aware of how your body feels. Take notice of how your arms, shoulders, knees, neck feel. Breathe into any body part that needs extra energy to help it to relax and let go.

4. Take notice of how your clothes feel on your body.

5. Notice how your foot feels when it's on or off, the floor/ground. Walk meaningfully as you allow your focus to centre your mind and quiet your thoughts.

6. How do your hips feel? Swing them a little and let your shoulders sway gently. Stretch your tongue out! How does this feel?

7. Become aware of how your whole body is feeling as you walk slowly and intentionally. Ask the Universe, and the Earth below you to bring you new energy, inspiration and peace. Allow the energy of the sky/cosmos to cleanse you and to transform any concerns you have into harmony and clarity.

8. As you walk, breathe in the energy of the Earth and the crystals that live in the earth. Allow the crystal energy to rise up through the soles of your feet into your body and aura, and then pour out through your crown chakra, at the top of your head, into the space around you.

9. Breathe in the energy of the sky, planets and cosmos. Allow this vast energy to come into your crown chakra at the top of your head and fill your body with healing and love. Breathe out the energy into the earth below you.

10. As you walk let your mind be still or repeat loving thoughts such as "I am at peace". "I am full of joy", "I trust that all is happening for a divine reason." "I feel the earth and sky filling me with wonderful energy and vibrations."

11. Scan your body from the soles of your feet to the top of your head and be aware of how your body feels. Send love to every cell in your body. (We have trillions of cells in our body!)

12. Enjoy **Walking In Love** and your Soul will feel more alive and present.

Mel's Mother-in-Law

My client Mel told me her mother-in-law's negative energy was affecting the relationship she had with her partner. Not only was Mel feeling down about the conflict, she felt uncomfortable in her own house and couldn't shake the feeling that negative elements were around her.

I could see psychically that there was heavy energy in one bedroom of her house. I tuned into the room and found a spirit who was feeding off the fear and stress of the people living in the house. We did a clearing and I gave Mel some sage to help clear the energy in her home.

Mel was happy to do a visualisation to also help her relationship with her mother-in-law. Mel closed her eyes as I began the visualisation. I was shown a beautiful grotto with divine spiritual energy. Afterwards Mel told me that her mother-in-law had been abused by her parents and, at the tender age of 10 and had been put into a foster home. There the abuse had continued at a higher level. Having compassion and understanding for someone else's story can help us to resolve issues in a more healing way.

Visualisation and Self-hypnosis

Visualisation is when we create images in our mind. Our subconscious does not know the difference between what's real and what's not so when we visualise we are having a conversation with our subconscious mind.

Imagine a lemon, cut it in half and imagine you biting into the lemon. Most people will have a reaction when they read this. Can you feel your body and mind react even though you only thought about eating a lemon? Your body thought it was real because you were thinking it. Just imagining you're eating a lemon causes saliva to be released in your mouth because the subconscious thought it was real. What you imagine impacts our body right here, right now because it thinks it's real. So what are you telling yourself? If scientist Bruce Lipton is right by stating our subconscious is 1 million times greater than our conscious then, imagine how powerful the superconscious is!

Self-Hypnosis

What is self-hypnosis?

It is said that all hypnosis is self-hypnosis, as you are in control and you allow yourself to go into that dreamy, yet powerful, state. Hypnosis is a process that helps you "talk" between your mind and body. You get to talk to your subconscious through images and feelings. In hypnosis your mind goes into a trance which is a daydream-like state.

Self-Hypnosis happens when we concentrate and focus. It's about how we program our brain and mind to do things. It's a natural thing we all do. We do it when we are imagining what to wear, who to buy a gift for or what to eat next. Every thought and message we send to ourselves is a form of hypnosis. We hypnotise ourselves by what we see, hear and view around us. As a result self-hypnosis has been used to change patterns and habits.

I have used visualisations on family members who were going through a challenging time and the results have been astonishing. A relative saw me about a work problem they were having with their boss. I asked them to visualise themselves standing in front of their boss. I had them tune into the energy of their boss and see colour around them. I then had my relative tune into the feelings of their boss and they were surprised that they could sense their boss was struggling with work and home pressures. This visualisation gave my relative more compassion about the stress their boss was under. We also sent healing energy to the whole workplace and visualised the workplace as being cleansed and purified.

How can self-hypnosis help me?

Self-hypnosis can help you by focusing your attention. Hypnosis allows you to go to a deeper level of your being. This level allows you to activate healing, achieve goals and dreams and change habits and emotional states such as fears and anxieties.

The more you do self-hypnosis the more creative your mind becomes and the deeper you will go. I now drop into a deep state much quicker than I used to. This is because I meditate more often so my mind and body are used to getting into a relaxed state. I also naturally go into a light trance when I am doing hypnotherapy, readings or healings with clients. Reducing my intake of sugar over the years has helped my nervous system to relax more too.

Sugar is stimulating so less sugar in the body means it's more relaxed and therefore more receptive to going into a calm state. Drugs, alcohol and stimulants such as coffee may affect the ability to go into certain levels of trance.

How does hypnosis work?

When you watch a movie and are relaxed you become less aware of distractions. This allows you to be more open to suggestion/ideas so that you can heal, create what you want or allow your inner wisdom to give you messages.

Note: *If you are concerned about doing self-hypnosis please see your health professional.*

What is a trance?

A trance is a heightened state of attention where your body is more open to suggestions and ideas. Everyone has experienced trance states many times such as in a daydream when the mind wanders off. When we watch TV we go into a trance. What messages and images is the television program putting into your mind and thoughts?

How often should I do self-hypnosis?

Self-hypnosis works best when you have time and space to relax. Do not try to go into a hypnotic state when you are driving a car or doing other activities where you need to be concerned about your safety.

Public Speaking

I often do public speaking in front of groups ranging from 5 people up to larger groups of 500. To help me with public speaking I do self-hypnosis several days before the event. I do this by visualising myself in a relaxed place. I then imagine standing up in front of the audience. I see myself feeling relaxed smiling and enjoying myself. This simple technique helps me programme my mind and body to respond in a certain way when I am public speaking.

Exercise: Self Hypnosis (Autohypnosis)

Trance/ Breathing – Close eyes and take 8 deep belly breaths. Breathe slowly in and out. Feeling more calm and serene with each out breath.

Induction/Relaxation

1. Imagine a beautifully designed staircase that has ten steps going down to a natural sanctuary. You stand at the top of the staircase. As you walk down the steps begin to count from 10 to 1 allowing yourself to gently relax deeper and deeper with each step you take. You begin to step down the staircase feeling more and more relaxed as you breathe out. Counting down now...

   10...Relax your face and jaw and tongue

   9...Relax your forehead, eyes and eyelids

   8...Relaxing the back of your neck and shoulders

   6...Relax your chest and ribs

   5...Relax your belly, liver and stomach

   4...Relax your hips and buttocks

   3...Relax your legs, knees and ankles

   2...Relax your toes and feet

   1...Here you are in this gorgeous natural environment.

2. You see a long path ahead of you. You feel your feet on the ground. You feel light and free. You are in awe of your surroundings. The sounds, the colours, the smells of this natural environment.

3. Find a place to lie and rest. Allow your whole body to go deeply relaxed. Cover yourself with a blanket if you wish, and use a pillow for your head. Feel relaxed and at peace. You feel so comfortable, loved and secure.

Suggestions/Goals

While you are relaxing and lying down in this natural sanctuary you can imagine, ask and affirm what you want and desire in your life. Your imagination, and deeply relaxed state, will help you to connect with your subconscious and superconscious. Allow this to be gentle and fun for you. Be gentle and loving towards yourself.

Ask:

Ask your higher self and Guide some questions you would like answered. Answers may come straight away or within a few days. Answers may come to you via a dream, a song, a person or a feeling.

Come out of the Trance/ Self-hypnosis:

By counting 1 to 10 as you proceed back up the stairs.

Step 1 As you approach this step you feel deeply grateful for this experience

Step 2 Feeling confident

Step 3 Excited about your direction ahead

Step 4 Feeling calmer and happier

Step 5 Feeling more devoted to self

Step 6 Feeling empowered to make a difference

Step 7 Feeling content and strong

Step 8 Feeling in Love with life

Step 9 Feeling compassionate and caring to self and others

Reaching Step 10 Feeling alert, alive, wonderful fully present. Open your eyes and smile!

Tip: You can use different environments such as a beach, a crystal cave or a white temple. Experiment and see how that affects your self-hypnosis. Be creative and imaginative!

I have found visualisations and self-hypnosis incredibly powerful. They go hand in hand as they both work well together to get effective results. Science has proven that our brain does change when we do, and think, different things.

CHAPTER 5

Spirits, Guides & Higher Beings

There are always Guides around you. One or two main guides will be assigned to you from birth. They will connect with you more if you call them in and connect with them. They love to assist and support you and they can have a good sense of humour!

I usually see main guides standing directly behind a person's head. Sometimes I clairvoyantly see shadows, while other times the guides appear more clearly to me. Most times I sense the guides gender while other times I do not. I may ask telepathically, in my mind, for the spirit or guide to show themselves more clearly to me.

Different guides may come into your energy field at certain times in your life, depending on what is happening to you. Loved ones who have crossed over can also be guides also. When I have a client sitting in front of me I may see their departed loved ones standing beside them. Generally, the mother's side of the family will appear near the left side of your body while the father's relatives appear on the right side of your body.

Exercise: Connecting with Guides Meditation

Let's guide you into a light trance.

1. Close your eyes and get comfy.

2. Breathe ten times deeply into your belly. Allow each breath to sink you into a deeply relaxed state.

3. Imagine you're sitting in a magical cave filled with crystals, crystalline energies and sensational luminous colours around you. This magical cave will help you to lift your vibration, open your third eye and heighten your intuitive senses. Take yourself to this magical cave whenever you want to connect and see your guides.

4. Ask three times for a Divine being, who loves you unconditionally, to step closer to you. Do you feel a shift in energy around you? You may feel tingles or feel like something is lightly touching your face or head. That's the spirit worlds way to connect with you and let you know they are around you.

5. Keep doing this exercise and watch how your connection with the Spirit realm grows. It's a beautiful and fascinating experience.

Be patient. Persistence pays off. Over time you may see totem animals appear, as well as other beings, who want to connect with you. In my magic cave I see different animals depending on what is going on in my life at the time. An elephant may appear to give me strength or a bird may appear to tell me to fly high and to spread my wings.

Energy Tip

Remember that toxic substances like alcohol and drugs can make your body and aura imbalanced. Foods such as sugar or junk food can make it more of a challenge for your soul to anchor correctly to your body. Unnatural foods with preservatives and chemicals in them may make you feel tired, flat, light headed and ungrounded. It's best to only ingest substances that are natural for the human body. Your body finds it easier to digest foods such as fruit, vegetables, nuts and seeds.

Fluids like herbal teas are healing for your body and soul. If your physical body is nourished and strong then your spirit will be connected to your physical being in a more grounded way. Occasional treats are OK for the body to have. If you are eating well 90% of the time then the occasional treat food will be better tolerated by the body.

ID – Calling card

You can ask your guide, or spirit, to give you a sign when they are around. Do a meditation like the *Connecting with Guides* meditation above.

Go into the magical cave and ask your guide to show you what they look like. Ask them for an ID that helps you identify them. For example; you can ask them to show you a pink ball or a green stone when they are around you. Open your psychic senses and see how they let you know of their ID or calling card. It could be a colour, a picture, a sound. My Italian grandfather crossed over at the ripe old age of 101 many years ago. His ID to me is a butterfly. The butterfly may appear as a real one that flutters close to me. I connect and commune with the energy of the butterfly and ask for its message. Other times a butterfly may appear in my vision to let me know that my grandfather is nearby guiding me and sending me love.

Soul Guides are there from birth and their job is to watch over you. Call on them to guide you and to show you signs to help you along your path.

Gatekeeper Guides protect you and only allow the right energy into your space. Gatekeeper guides help bring through the right spirit connections especially in mediumship. A gatekeeper has many roles.

They are like advanced guides who help you with tuning into psychic information, give you confidence and protect you. They help bring the right spirits to you so you can link with them.

Healing guides assist and come to us in times of need. I have had challenging times in my life when I have felt spirit support me as I could feel their energy around me. One time it felt like a spiritual hug as I felt a warm embrace around me. When spirit is around you may feel a tap on the head or a vibration on your body. Guides may work on your body to help rebalance your energies. Just ask as they are always willing to assist you.

Angels (or Devas) are Higher beings who also like to support and gently guide us. They honour our free will as they know we have the final decision in making choices in our life.

Maria's Angel

I was doing half-hour readings at a busy psychic fair. Maria, aged 68, had booked in for a reading. She said her friend had given her the reading as a gift. Maria was European and had a strong accent. She sat down at my table while I shuffled the tarot cards. I saw, behind Maria's right shoulder, a tall, green loving energy. It was ethereal, beautiful and serene. I was looking at an Angelic Being. I shared my vision with Maria to which she responded, "Of course I have an Angel around me, I pray every day to my Angels." I then noticed a cord going from the Angel to Maria's abdomen. I then said to Maria "I feel the Angel has been helping you with healing around your tummy area and back." Maria said she'd had an operation on her abdomen and lower back and was told she would not walk again. Maria continued to pray every day for a miracle. "The Angels helped me to walk again," Maria shared. The doctors were surprised that she healed so well yet Maria said she was not surprised. She knew her faith and prayers would get her through.

Faery Folk are elemental and nature spirits which connect us to the natural forces around us. Faery Folk are usually directly related to one of the main elemental energies of Nature such as Water, Earth, Wood (Trees) and Sky.

FAERIES are usually around to remind us of our responsibility to care for and treat the Earth with kindness. They may also be there to remind us that we need to reconnect to one of our elemental resources. Fire Faeries like Salamanders may be telling us to be more fiery and go after what we desire, a Water spirit such as an Undine tells us to listen to our strong emotions and perhaps the need for more water in our life and diet. Sylphs are faeries of the Air and they resonate with freedom and clear thinking. When a Faery appears to you, sit quietly with them and enjoy their energy, allowing yourself to intuitively understand their message to you.

Elementals are spirits of the elements and that's why they are called elementals! Elementals include gnomes, sylphs, salamanders, undines and leprechauns. I clairvoyantly see elementals around people who love nature and spend time walking, gardening or other activities where they commune with the natural environment.

Gnomes are linked to the element of earth. **Rock faeries** are also called gnomes. These faeries live above and below the ground.

Sylphs are linked to the element of air. They may radiate golden white sparkles as well. I also see them clairvoyantly with various colours around them. They have a very light energy and they may have a high-pitched sound emanating from them. Ask them to show themselves to you and observe what you sense.

Undines are water spirits or water faeries. Undines are linked to the element of water.

Salamanders are linked to the element of fire.

Tree spirits live around trees. They may look like a shape or appear like a shadowy figure near a tree. They are part of the tree's energy and can be quite chatty! When I open my third eye and ask to see tree spirits I am shown different beings around trees. Sometimes it may look like a feminine energy that stands near the tree. Other times I have seen a male energy with a face that has leaves on it  near a tree! Ask them for information. Tree spirits seem to protect the tree and guard it. I love the way the shamans call trees "tree people". Also ask the tree to show you any nature spirits, elementals and other energies that belong to the tree.

Psychic Protection

It is important to protect yourself when starting to enter into psychic work. The most powerful psychic protection is the gold and white light. Some people find the violet flame also powerful as well. Use the violet flame by imagining its energy enveloping you, then imagine it's extending out into the space around you and then the whole planet. The best psychic protection is also your health and thoughts.

Good health protects your cells and your spirit body. Guard what thoughts you say to yourself. Also feed your body high-vibration foods that keep your aura strong and resilient. Reduce acidic foods and substances which drain your energy and body.

Crystal Bubble of Protection

At the beginning of a visualisation with a client I will ask them to imagine that the room is filled with coloured energy or huge coloured crystals. Sometimes my eyelids will flicker as a sign that the energy vibration has risen. Imagining that I'm standing in the middle of the most magical divinely coloured crystal is fabulous for protection and enhancing energy.

If I'm giving psychic Reiki to a person I imagine crystals around myself and around the client. This helps shift the vibration in the room and in our souls.

Prayer/Affirmation Protection

A Simple prayer to do at the beginning of a session or before you go out into the world can be surprisingly effective.

Here is a simple version or, you can create your own prayer:

Please protect my aura and spirit in this situation. May I enjoy the experience ahead of me and may all people involved feel connected and aligned to their higher purpose.

Working with Spirit Guides

Over the years, I have tried different ways to tune into clients better. I found that when I called in the client's own guide, and higher self, I would then see an energy standing behind the client. Other times I saw my own spirit guide guiding and talking to me. With practice you will get to know and differentiate which is which. It's beautiful to have a client sit in front of you, as you look at their aura and chakras, and watch the colour that emanates from their gorgeous soul.

Ask from your heart, to see and sense the person's guide as well as your own, to help in the session. You will tune into the guide's energy and vibration. They will start to communicate to you through your Clair senses as the spirit world will know you are ready to interact with them.

Shamanic Indian Guide

Jess came to me for a Reiki healing. I tuned into her aura and saw the colours blue and green around her. I noticed an Indian Guide behind Jess wearing a shamanic type dress. I told Jess what I had seen, "I have been told that before," Jess replied.

As I was giving Jess Reiki I again saw this Shamanic Indian Guide near her feet. The guide was hitting a drum. My head started to move from side-to-side signalling to me the shift in energy. Some healer's hands vibrate when the energy vibration in the room has increased or, the client may notice a change in temperature. I went up into my Soul star chakra (9th chakra) to see if I could view more. I could see Spirits working on her tummy where she had had several bowel operations. This is called psychic surgery. Psychic surgery is a form of healing that involves physical or spiritual surgery. Different countries practise it in different ways. Psychic surgery to me is where I clairvoyantly see, or I intuitively sense, that there are spirits in the room who lovingly assist and help in the healing. I may see energy, or spirit hands near a chakra, such as the sacral chakra where the spirit is helping the client to heal their digestive issues.

Exercise: Open Third Eye

1. Relax and breathe deeply. Keep your physical eyes closed through-out this exercise if possible.

2. Imagine, as you breathe in and out that a White Golden Light of energy is filling up inside your body and the space around you. Imagine this White Golden Light of energy is calming, soothing and protecting you with Divine love and essence.

3. Now take your attention back to the area in-between your eyebrows. You may sense it feels different to before. The White Golden Light of energy will have helped your third eye to gently expand and activate.

4. Ask your 3rd eye to open. You may feel something happening around the area in-between your eyebrows, such as tingles, warmth or pressure, which is your body responding to your request.

5. Now imagine that you are opening the door to your house, you walk in and you notice what you see. You look around at the furni-ture and you notice the colours, the light, the shapes.

6. Now imagine that you are in a movie theatre. You are watching a big red screen but you notice that it changes to a silvery blue colour.

Now it's different shades of blue. You now see your bedroom on the screen. Imagine yourself walking into your room. Ask to be shown other images on your screen. Take notice and be aware of any other colours, shapes, smells, sounds or movement that you "see."

7. Now ask to be shown something on the screen that happened yesterday and see what it looks like. Ask for the images to be clearer and more focused if you require more clarity.

8. Ask what will happen tomorrow and see what comes up on your screen. Keep practising to strengthen your third eye area.

Advanced Exercise:

1. Open your 3rd eye energy and look at people's auras around you. You'll be surprised what colours and shapes are around all living things. Try this on plants and flowers. You may notice the colours change with people emotional states.

2. Practise your 3rd eye vision by looking at trees. Maybe you will see tree spirits, elemental beings or faeries around them or, you may notice colours, vibrations or movement.

CHAPTER 6

Mediumship, Symbols & Dreams

"The greatest spiritual path any of us can follow is the one that attempts to make the unconscious conscious."[12]

There are differences between a psychic and a medium. A psychic is not a medium, but a medium is a psychic.

Psychics tune into the energy of people, or objects, by using their clair senses. Psychics use their sense of intuition and psychic ability to gather information for the person being read.

Mediums act as a bridge between the spiritual and the physical world. Mediums tap into spirits and family members who have crossed over using their psychic and intuitive abilities. Some mediums also connect with spirit guides and higher beings. Mediums may energetically merge with the energy of the spirit being so they can get a more powerful connection with that realm of energy.

---

12 Wolf, Linda (2009) *Shamanic Breathwork* (p.127) Bear & Company, Vermont.

Mental Mediums communicate with spirits through the use of telepathy. Spirits will link or merge with their energy. Mental mediums tune-in by using their "clairs" such as "hearing" (clairaudience), "seeing" (clairvoyance), "knowing" (claircognizance) and "feeling" (clairsentience).

Psychics

Extra-sensory perception (ESP) means beyond the senses. Psychics tap into their natural ESP senses to gain insight to people, events or situations that would otherwise not be available to the normal range of senses.

Psychics and mediums have trained themselves to see beyond this physical realm and are open to receiving messages and insights using their heightened senses. We are born with eyes, ears and a heart but we also are born with the ability to see, hear and feel beyond this realm. The more we meditate the more we can tap into these subtle energies.

Psychics and mediums use their extra-sensory perceptions to gain insight to people, events or situations. They tap into the superconscious to gain information and insight. One of my psychic teachers said that the spirit world will only pass on information that would help us to evolve. They do not create fear or pass on things that would block or impede our development. The spirit world and superconscious is incredibly intelligent and they want us to move forward with love, wisdom, knowledge and faith.

Exercise: Intuition Cross

1. Imagine that there is a beautiful cross shape. The horizontal line goes from one ear to the other and the vertical line of the cross travels from the area in-between your eyebrows (third eye) and down to your heart.

2. Surround the cross with golden white light and thank the cross for connecting your higher chakras and activating your intuitive areas of your Being.

3. Close your eyes and be in silence as you tune into this divine energy and its presence. As you focus on the divine cross, ask it to activate and show you a colour, images or pattern on it. It may show you leaves growing, a colour, or it may even have sounds.

4. If you feel comfortable, activate it during the day and see what happens to your intuitive senses!

Earth School

Sometimes we are tested so that we can learn, grow and develop. I remember when I was studying for one of my bachelor degrees. I received distinctions in some subjects whereas in other subjects it was more challenging. I also had to resit an exam that I had failed. Redoing the exam test was challenging but it made me relearn the material and therefore have a deeper understanding of it. It felt really good when I finally did pass! Sometimes life tests us to make us stronger and more resilient. We may leave a relationship because it doesn't suit us. We think by leaving the relationship we leave the problem but sometimes the same challenge will reappear in another relationship. I feel we get tested until we pass then we move onto another challenge. This earth plane is a place like school. We go to the next grade when we have a good understanding of that level's concepts. I meet some people who do not pass the tests because they are stubborn and dig in their heels instead of seeing the gift in the lesson. They fail to understand and continue to blame others, be a victim, so they stay on that same level and do not progress.

My Soul Healing

Decades ago I ended up in court with an abusive ex-partner. Police orders were involved. It was an incredibly challenging time. It took me several years to heal from the betrayal and the hurt. The situation lead me to self-help courses, spiritual groups and healers in the search to find peace, healing and happiness.

Over time my heart began to thaw from the sadness and pain. I realised that forgiveness would set me free. I looked at my own behaviour in the relationship and decided to reflect on why it all occurred. I knew bitterness would consume my soul and my mindset. I wanted to be set free.

I decided to learn how to better master my own emotions and mindset. I ended up having a respectful relationship with my ex. I rarely see him now but when I do I feel joy.

I am glad we met to walk through the fire of change and to come out the other end triumphant and free. I am glad the universe put us together so that we could play out the themes/patterns in our lives, learn to overcome them and find resolution and peace.

I realised that when I felt compassion for myself I could also feel it towards others. Each relationship that comes our way is a teacher and helps us to know more about ourselves.

When we do not choose love in our decision making we usually end up hurting ourselves. Sometimes we may be addicted to drama and negativity. If we are driven by these toxic emotions we need to work out how to substitute these with emotions that are fulfilling and passionate. If you make decisions based on ego, control or anger rather than love and compassion the outcomes will not be positive for you.

It's time to be a role model for others and do things differently. Hate breeds hate. Anger breeds anger. Love breeds love. What are we going to model to our children? To our neighbours? I have seen clients who live for years with bitterness, anger and despair. This heavy energy seeps into their cells, their bones and their mind. By holding on tight to this righteous behaviour we hurt our essence, our being. Creative thinking brings creative outcomes.

By forgiving someone it does not mean we suddenly believe what occurred was OK. But it means we are able to let go of that person or situation. By holding onto the negative feelings and anger towards the person we are allowing them to continue to control us and keep us captive.

Psychic Antenna

Psychics and mediums receive communication from the spirit world via images, words, feelings, sounds. A psychic antenna helps to gain more information from the spirit realms. It's like a TV or wi-fi picking up data and converting it into the image or words you see on your magic screen in your third eye. Sometimes psychics and mediums may need to ask the client to help decipher the meaning especially if it is very cryptic! Other times, if I see a symbol I am unsure of, I will ask telepathically what does it mean. Use all your senses to interpret what they are trying to communicate to ensure you give the best possible translation to your client.

Turn on your psychic antenna by consciously saying in your mind that you would like to see beyond this realm. The spirit world replies by allowing you to see, hear and feel more. We need to focus and connect with the energy just like if a person was speaking to us. If we relax and concentrate we are more likely to absorb the information they are telling us.

Intuitive Muscle

Intuitive insight is when we get a flash of knowing or, we sense something really strongly such as who's calling on the phone or we seem to know what the outcome of something will be. Sometimes it comes out of the blue. Intuition helps inspires us to be creative and also gives us ideas and impulses for what we need to do. Intuition can also guide us not to do something. Our intuitive gut can be a barometer for whether we go ahead and do something or not. The gut has a lot of nerve endings so it is able to tap into the unconscious part of us that communicates with us via feelings. Like psychic senses, our intuition connects to a more subtle frequency of communication between us and, the all-knowing higher realms. Intuition grows stronger and stronger the more we listen to it. Intuition is like a muscle – the more you use it the more it grows!

Empaths

Empathy is when we put ourselves in other people's shoes. Empathy is when we are aware of others feelings but we are not lost in them. Sympathy, on the other hand, is when we feel sad for another. With sympathy we sometimes can get lost in the persons grief or emotions as we feel so sad for them.

We all can feel empathy, but some people have a higher sensitivity and these people are known as empaths. They are highly attuned to the feelings of others and can usually pick up on how complete strangers are feeling without even speaking to them.

Symbol Language

The spirit world uses symbols to communicate to us. Psychics use different symbols in their readings to help them interpret what's happening in a client's life. For example, a wedding ring symbolises to me that a person is married or in a committed relationship. A black ring shows divorce or relationship issues.

Psychic Symbols

One day I was connecting with Beth's grandma who had crossed over. I told her I saw hands together in prayer position and rosary beads around them. Beth cried and said, "we buried my nanna with rosary beads wrapped around her hands."

Below is a chart of some of the symbols I have come across when doing psychic medium readings. I am always amazed at how clever spirit is and the way they try their best to communicate with me via symbols, which is a universal language! **Note:** your symbols may be different to mine depending on the spirit or energy that comes through. Make a list of your own symbols.

Anna's Symbol Chart:

Table 6.1

	Word	Symbols & Meaning
A	**Anxiety**	Anxiety symbol may appear as two clenched hands holding a twisted rope.
B	**Baby**	Blue bub means boy baby coming. Pink bub means a baby girl waiting to come in.
	Buying or spending	Symbol of money leaving hands.
	Back	A symbol of a body bending forward at the waist may mean client has a sore lower back.
	Brain	I remember seeing an image of a head. Half the brain was white, and half the brain was black and client said she had been diagnosed with bipolar disorder.

C	Cakes	Symbols of cakes are fun to see as they indicate a birthday or celebration coming up. If you see two cakes this may mean two celebrations or twins' birthdays. A pink cake may indicate a female birthday whereas a boy is blue. A bronze-coloured cake is usually an anniversary of some sort.
	Cigarette	If I see an image of a cigarette this may indicate the person has a bad habit of some sort. It may be smoking OR some other habit such as overeating or drinking to excess.
	Cash register & coins	I was surprised once when I saw an image of a cash register full of coins! I told the clients about this image floating near her head. She smiled and said she had recently received a large lump sum of money from a payout.
	Cards	If I see playing cards or, tarot/oracle cards, it usually means the client is intuitive and to use cards so they can tap into their natural intuition.
	Chocolate	A symbol of a block of chocolate indicates client needs to be careful about the amount of sugar and junk food they are eating.
D	Drink	Over the years I have learnt a glass with white colour in it indicates milk. Clear liquid is water, yellow is herbal tea, orange is alcohol, brown is coffee or soft drink.
	Digging with a shovel	This reveals someone who is a hard worker.
	Dream	If I see a person with a thought bubble coming from their head it may highlight their dreams.
E	Envelopes	Shows communication and messages.
F	Fridge	A fridge can sometimes mean a person is a bit cold and frosty but one day after telling the client I had seen a fridge she said "My parents just gave me one for my 30th!"
	Face	One day I saw a large face with make-up on it. The image was suspended mid-air and looked like a painting. I shared this image with the client and she said, "My daughter painted a portrait of herself. How did you know!"
	French Stick	I saw a French Stick and told my client to which she replied, "yes, my daughter's going to Paris soon."

G	Gold star	Good Luck coming your way! Job well done.
H	Hands	Movement means plumber/trade job or likes playing guitar.
	Handkerchief	My client said she was not sad but I kept seeing a white hanky which symbolises sadness and tears. I told her this and all of a sudden she burst out crying. We discussed her grief and the client healed well.
J	Jewel	I saw a ruby gem once and the client said her grandma's name was Ruby! I saw a ring with a blue stone in it and the client said she had her grandmother's blue ring.
L	Light	If I see an image of a bedroom with a lamp beside the bed, it usually means the person is up late at night.
M	Money	I was amused one day to see a watch on a wrist then a dollar note on the palm. I realised it meant watch your money! Money coming to you may look like money notes falling down. Dark-coloured money means overspending.
N	Numbers	I remember seeing a large number 13 floating mid-air. I was doing a psychic phone reading with a client from England. The client told me she had a number 13 tattoo on her wrist! Numbers may reveal house numbers, someone's age or birthdates.
	Nuts	Nuts represent protein (amino acids) so it may be spirit's way of saying person needs more protein in their diet.
P	People	I remember once seeing rows of people behind a person. The client had MS and I told her I felt that generations before a family member had nervous system issues too. Client revealed that her great-grandmother did have those health issues.
	Picnic mat and food	Relax. Take a chill pill, go on a picnic and relax!
	Phone	Call someone or phone the Spirit world!
	Popcorn	Unexpected things happening which will excite you.
R	Radio	Symbol of communication.

S	Sing	See an image of mouth open and lips moving.
	Sniff	Spirit made this sniffing sound in my ear. Client said they had sniffles lately due to a cold.
T	Ticket	Image of a rectangle shape with number and words on part of it. Client said they had been to the theatre the night before.
	Teeth	If I see teeth chewing/grinding this means the person is stressed and some clients say they grind their teeth in their sleep.
	Tie	Going somewhere formal; see a professional or an important decision to make. Client was going to see a lawyer about a will issue she was concerned about.
	Tablets	Green tablets represent herbs, whereas white tablets usually mean prescribed medication.
	Toilet Roll	This one's funny. I remember seeing it one day and was perplexed until I realised it meant letting go and releasing the past!
	Toothpaste	Cleansing is required or see a dentist.
W	Wedding	Image of a white wedding dress indicates a wedding. A black wedding dress may mean relationship issues or divorce.
	Waterfall	May show situation needs cleansing and healing.

Mediumship with Joe

Joe arrived in my office. He had brown hair and a warm smile. Joe was 48-years-old. He sat in a comfy chair in my office. Joe said his friend had recommended me to him.

As usual, I begin with a light chitchat to make us both feel relaxed and comfortable. I asked Joe about his day. He calmly said that he had been busy. I took the opportunity to look at his aura and any spirits around him. If I open up my third eye then I am able to tune into the person's energy and aura. (I had done 5–10 mins of yoga and a short meditation before Joe had arrived so my chakras were filled with more energy.)

"I have a short woman here," I said. I shared some initials but he was not sure who the lady was. I continued passing information from this spirit about Joe's health, his interests and his family. He responded that the details were correct. I then said that Spirit was showing me some letters and they were Ca...

I said I wasn't sure of the rest of the word.

"It's my Mum!" He cried out. "Her name was Cathy!"

Tears rolled down his cheeks. I continued passing on messages to Joe from his mum who wanted to share details about his wife, children and his sweet tooth!

I saw an image of a cat but felt it was a stuffed toy rather than a real one. "I see a cat on your daughter's bed but I don't feel it's a real cat," I stated.

"You're right" he said, "my daughter loves her toy cat."

He cried as I told him his Mum was around and that lights in the home may flash on and off. "Yes!" he exclaimed, "that's what's been happening!"

I also read Joe's palms and noticed marks which symbolised his natural mystical abilities. He looked at me and said, "Well I'll have to admit something to you, Anna. I heard my Mum call my name. I was in the kitchen, several months after she passed away, and I clearly heard her voice say my name and no-one else was in the house!"

Sacred Crossing Over

I have had several clients who were distressed after a psychic, or astrologer, had told them the year that a family member may die. Clients can end up worrying for years after receiving this news and the predictions are often inaccurate. The spirit world does not want us, as healers and therapists, to instil fear and anxiety into our clients. We are there to support, uplift and guide them.

Platform Mediumship

Platform mediumship is when a medium stands in front of a group of people. The medium will tap into spirits and then share the information they have received. The medium will link with a spirit energy and then connect with a person in the audience to pass on any messages they receive.

I studied platform mediumship many years ago in a Spiritual circle I attended. I remember standing up in front of a hall connecting to spirit guides and deceased loved ones. There was a professional Medium there who told me that I could do platform Mediumship professionally if I wanted to. What I didn't realise at the time was that mediumship takes practice, inner confidence and the ability to relax, and trust, as the Spirit world is in control and you have to follow their lead.

I did many courses in mediumship so I could expand my knowledge and connection with the Spirit world. But standing in front of people can be scary so it prevents a lot of mediums doing platform mediumship. Before doing platform I would practise at home, with family members, doing mini-platform sessions. I would stand up in my lounge room and tune into their loved ones and asked them for confirmation. It's a great way to practise and to get used to standing up in front of people.

Several times a year I do mediumship at a local Spiritual Church. This Church is fabulous at it allows mediums with different styles to do their thing. I do have a different style and even though I have been trained in a variety of Mediumship styles I do what flows best for me and I teach my mediumship students to do the same. At times the connections are amazing and the feedback is great. Other times the links do not feel as strong and I do my best afterwards to reflect on how I could improve.

I feel, as a Psychic medium, that we can all have our off days but we need to be honest, as mediums, about what we can and can't do as we are all gifted in certain areas. Mediumship ability is a skill and, like most other skills, it takes dedication, effort and commitment to give justice to it.

Piggybacking in Mediumship means that a few spirits may come through at the same time. They may be from the same family or, have passed over with similar conditions. I was reading for a client whose mother had passed away a few months prior. I was passing messages on from the mother when I saw a younger brighter energy overlap the mother's presence. Apparently the client's dearly departed sister thought it was now her turn to connect. She also passed on lovely messages for my client.

Linking In is when two mediums work together to link into the same spirit to pass on messages.

Mediumship with Joan

Joan arrived at my clinic one spring afternoon. She had seen me several times for a Naturopathic session but was now keen for a Psychic reading.

Joan sat down at my reading table. I visualised a white colour around her (as this helps me to "see" spirits around people.) I asked for spirit to show themselves to me.

A dark haired, thin lady appeared to me. This lady showed me the letters **Gi** and **Jo** so I shared this information with Joan. My client said "Theres no-one in my family with these initials." I continued tuning into this lady to get more evidence.

I then remarked that the lady in spirit was coughing so I sensed that Joan has been unwell. Joan confirmed that she was getting over a bad cough. I continued on saying that "the lady in spirit shows me that your son has a cold at the moment too."

"Oh yes he does! I know who this lady is!" Joan exclaimed. "It's my mum's Mother! Her name was Giovanna which in Italian means Joan and I was named after her." This Italian grandmother was a jovial and funny spirit and I enjoyed communicating with her energy.

"She was known to be a character," laughed Joan. I continued tuning into this lovely spirit.

"She tells me you are planning a trip in June."

"Oh that's funny" Joan said, "I was only booking the motel last night!"

Giovanna continued with messages of love but also some stern messages to help Joan with her health and marriage and some of the steps she had to take to improve her life.

Joan said she felt someone had been around her but that the reading made her realise that she could connect with her Spirit more and could call on her grandmother for help and assistance when she needed it.

Exercise: Mediumship Power Up (Energy Up)

Power up is a name that is connected to Mediumship. This term has been around for a while. It means to meditate and increase your energy, or power, so that you can tune in adequately to the spirit world. Power up enhances your vibration so that you may even feel tingles around you or a shift in energy. I know that meditating before I do a reading allows me to tap into the other realms much more effectively.

1. Take a big, deep breath in, hold it for a count of 6, then breathe out relaxing your shoulders, your head, your body and legs.
2. Repeat several times until you feel deeply relaxed, still and content.

3. Take another deep breath in and send love and peace, to your body, the world and to the cosmos. Let yourself relax even further.

4. Be aware of your thoughts as you continue to breathe deeply in and out. Ask your higher self and guides to help you to tap into the spirit world.

5. Take a moment to sense any messages, images, feelings, thoughts or words that they might share with you. The spirits know your intention is to have a two-way communication with them.

6. Relax and trust that the right information will come through for you.

Have fun with it as the more relaxed you are the more your senses will heighten and the more you will connect to the spirits' vibration and energy.

Exercise: Mediumship Questions to Ask

When you receive a connection with a spirit ask them the questions below telepathically, from your mind to their mind. This will help you to verify who is there.

I find some spirits do not verify themselves clearly. They just want to pop in and send pertinent information to my client. It's best to gently persist and ask the spirit for information so the client knows who is there. Sometimes the client does not recall who the spirit is. Sometimes they realise after the session is over and they may email me to say they did remember who the spirit was that was coming through with messages.

Practise on a spirit you know that has crossed over. Even if you know the answers you will be surprised at how the spirit communicates the answers to you. Write any information down if you wish. Remember to begin with a simple meditation (like the Mediumship Power Up above) as that will help you go into a deeply relaxed state so you are more receptive to the spirit world's language.

Questions:

1. What is your Relationship to the client?
2. What is your Name?
3. How did you cross over? i.e. fast or slow, your health, were you in hospital or at home? Was someone with you?
4. How many children did you have?
5. What was your occupation/ hobbies?
6. Do you have any significant marks?
7. Do you have any significant dates and events?
8. Do you have any significant memories?
9. Why are you communicating with us?
10. Are there other family members around you in spirit?
11. Can you validate any recent events my client is having so they know you are watching over them?
12. Any messages you would like to share?

Interpreting Dreams

In order to really understand the symbols that come to you during your dreams, it is important to write down any memories of your dreams as soon as possible upon waking. Your dream journal will help you to unlock the meanings of your dreams and how certain ideas, feelings and situations are communicated to you by your subconscious. Use a dream symbol book or find an online dream dictionary that can help you interpret your dreams. Remember your intuition is your best guide.

For decades, I have been having fun interpreting my dreams and the symbols that appear in them. I have many dream journals that I write my dreams in. Some messages are easy to understand while other messages are more cryptic. One year I had a dream that

I would get a new job on November 6th so I eagerly waited for this new job to manifest only to find out that it happened the year after!

Years ago, I had a dream that informed me to move on from my best friend. Sarah and I had a friendship for a few years. Our friendship was becoming unsettling and the boundaries were unhealthy. I saw so many good things in Sarah so I ignored my dream. Again the spirit world gave me another dream which symbolised that our friendship would be over in 6 month's time, and it was. I realised years later that the friendship had run its course and that it was time for both of us to move on in new directions. This hurt her and she found it hard to understand why it was happening but sometimes change is the best for all concerned.

I ran into Sarah several years later. We hugged and chatted. It was healing for both of us and I will always cherish the lovely times we had together.

Louise's Babies

My client Louise asked me to interpret her dream.

"I'm dreaming of babies but I don't want any as I'm thinking of leaving my boyfriend."

I told Louise that babies in a dream indicate new beginnings and new birth within one's self.

Louise did end up breaking up with her boyfriend. She bought her first home and began a new job. The baby dream was reflecting the new beginnings and new experiences that were to come into her life.

Dreaming of babies can also indicate new growth happening in one's life. Mind you, babies can also mean real babies.

Use your intuition to see if the image is symbolic or not. There is an increase in energy around the full moon so you may find you dream more then.

Nightmares can be a sign of your subconscious releasing inner fears. When you have nightmares, ask yourself what fears do you have that may need your attention to help alleviate them. Make sure you are eating well, as this will help balance your chakras, aura and therefore will balance your mind too.

Exercise: Your Own Psychic Symbols

Ask your Guides/Higher Self to show you symbols for these topics. If you have symbols for the areas below it will make it easier to communicate with a spirit world that communicates via symbols!

Table 6.2

Finance symbols for: Good, savings, debt, plans	**Yes** symbols are... **No** symbols are... Possibly/Wait symbols are...
Health symbols for: Good, concerns, food habits, liquids or drinks	**Job** symbols for: Occupation, Change career, new job, retired
Relationships: Married, Separated, Partnered, Seeking Love, Children, Baby	**House:** Renovations, moving, rent, own, live with

CHAPTER 7

Automatic Writing and Channelling

Automatic Writing

Automatic writing is a wonderful tool to use. You'll be surprised at the way information can be channelled through you. Automatic writing is where we allow higher wisdom to come through us as we use paper and pen to transcribe the information. There is a higher consciousness that is always streaming information about the past, present and future. Automatic writing allows us to tap into this amazing consciousness.

Rachael's Healing

Rachael had booked her first appointment with me. Before she arrived for her session I did some automatic writing. I relaxed and meditated then wrote down some information that flowed through me.

As I was writing I could see fleeting images of Rachael in the kitchen eating in the middle of the night. Rachael turned up for her appointment and sat down in my clinic chair. She told me she wanted to work on her weight issues. Rachael also confessed that she would get up in the middle of the night to obsessively snack.

The automatic writing accurately revealed the information as well as issues Rachael was having with her mother. In her session we discovered some deep subconscious issues that were causing Rachael to act in unusual ways. After some deep-healing sessions Rachael lost weight and began living a much healthier and balanced life.

Spirit messages

Sometimes Spirit messages and information come from outside our head and flow into our mind. Spirit messages may be stronger on one side of your head than the other. I find I receive most spirit messages from the right-hand side of my head although sometimes the left side of my head feels activated and buzzing with Spirit interaction and information.

When I'm doing automatic writing I feel the energy comes from a couple of inches away from my right ear and travels into my mind. The energy that comes through to me is very subtle, loving and gentle. I may receive pictures, images, knowingness or a gut feeling about what I need to write down.

When you let go and allow the flow of energy to come through, your mind and your intuition will be strong and powerful. If your busy monkey mind (beta) is on, then you may find your own thoughts are constantly in your head, wanting to take control and dominate. If so, I suggest you keep practising a couple of minutes a day where you take a deep breath, relax your body and allow yourself to go deeper and deeper into a place of quiet stillness.

Exercise: How to do Automatic Writing

Concentrate on a number, a word or, focus on your belly rising and falling. This will help you go into a slower alpha-brain wave pattern. Another good way to prepare before automatic writing, and channelling information, is to focus on your nostrils as air goes in and out of your body. A mantra or a word, is also a powerful way to settle the monkey mind and allows you to focus on slowing down and allowing the energies to come to you.

1. The best way to do automatic writing is to close your eyes and take 10 deep power breaths. This will allow your brain waves to slow and down and drop into an alpha/theta state.

2. Breathe in and out and allow your shoulders to relax. Continue to breathe in and out and allow a wave of happiness to spread over your body as your body smiles internally, feeling joy in its beautiful cells. Feel the subtle changes in your body as you allow this wave of joy and happiness to resonate through your Being. You are the master of your breath, your thoughts, your actions. How powerful is that? Allow your body to feel more and more relaxed. Do this deep breathing for 1 more minute.

3. Now concentrate on your third eye area in-between your eyebrows. Choose a word that you like such as peaceful, loving or calming and as you breathe in and out say that word slowly for example, Breathe in "Calm", breathe out "ing".

4. It's good to meditate for 5–15 minutes and then get out a piece of paper and ask "What do I need to know?"

5. Write down a question on a piece of paper questions such as "Tell me what I need to know about myself right now." Or something more specific such as, "Tell me about the holiday I am planning, how will it go?" Or, "I'm having a problem at work how should I resolve the situation?"

Now allow the higher guidance to come through your mind, from just outside your headspace, in a beautiful stream of energy. Allow this stream of thoughts, feelings and energy to enable you to write spirits' voice. At first it may seem like it's just coming from only you, but trust that your higher guidance is also helping and assisting you. The spirit world is keen to give you information that is accurate and pertinent to you.

The more you practice this exercise the more you become more skilled and adept at it. Remember that higher guidance speaks positively using encouraging words and advice.

If you feel any heavy energy coming through with negative statements, stop and ask it to go to the light by imagining that the ceiling, or the area above you, is a golden portal of light and ask any lower energies or entities to be released to the light with love. You could say to the heavy energy, "You are loved, please look to the light where you will be looked after. You are love, you are love, you are love." That will shift the heavy energy on and you will now know that those energies will be looked after and loved.

Be discerning about the energies you communicate with. Make sure the messages are inspiring, empowering and caring. Higher spirit energy will communicate to us with love even if they share with us something we need to improve on. Sometimes the energies are funny too, so be open to their sense of humour!

Imposter spirits

Some spirits are called imposter spirits as they pretend to be Higher Beings. The imposter spirits can be cheeky and like to pretend to be something they're not. Make sure you ask three times for higher beings, who love you unconditionally, to connect with you.

Channelling

We are all capable of reading energies, and vibrations, from many things around us, like people, flowers, crystals and pets. Tap into different energies and you'll be surprised by what you can pick up. I think the definition below is spot on as channelling is such a natural thing to do.

"Channelling is a natural form of communication between humans and angelic beings, nature spirits, non-physical entities, or even animals and pets. A channeller is very similar to a language translator or interpreter. They allow themselves to sense the non-verbal communication from another being and then translate it into human words."[13]

Channelling can be done in a room of people with everyone meditating and breathing deeply to centre and build up the energy. It is said the messages that come through the person, or Channel, are a combination of all the energies in the room and the messages will highlight what the people need to know and hear at that time.

The Chaneller has the ability to translate into words, the energy of the Spirit being channelled. Some Channellers use their body and allow another Spirit to take over until the channelling is completed and then the person returns to their body. Some Channellers say they're just energetically standing behind their physical body while the spirit has permission to use their body and voice box to pass on messages.

Other Channellers do not need to leave their body to channel messages, they just allow the messages to flow through them and they try not to affect the message with their own thoughts.

It's best to begin to channel with an experienced teacher or group. Asking for protection is necessary and your guides will step up to assist here. Altering your own energy body with drugs or alcohol will affect your vibration. You want to be sober and healthy to only attract Beings of light who want the best for all concerned.

---

13 https://www.crimsoncircle.com/Library/What-is-Channel

Listen to your heart and body. If you feel comfortable that the messages are loving and helpful then it should all be OK.

Channelling Pets

Mandy was distraught and grief stricken. Her beloved pet dog Zoro had passed way. Over several weeks I communicated and channelled information from Zoro who communicated to me via pictures, vibrations, feelings and words. Some people think dogs do not speak, but pets communicate in ways that they know will align with our understanding and consciousness.

Each week I would channel Zoro's energy and pass it onto Mandy. He told me things I could not have known such as how he died and what the vet did before he passed over. Zoro also communicated to me details about Mandy's children. He did all this to verify to Mandy that even though she could no longer pat or cuddle him he was still very much "alive" and was watching over her home and family. Zoro even told her where she would buy her next house and it was spot on!

Sometimes in the session I could see an outline of Zoro sitting next to me and sometimes he would sit on Mandy's lap and stand beside her leg. Mandy would feel his energy and vibration and could tap into his energy when she was at home. The bond between Mandy and Zoro was one of the most profound bonds I have ever seen. They had a soul-mate connection. Like all good relationships, their love brought about great wisdom, clarity and peace.

Exercise Anna's 4-Step Activation

Before doing any of the exercises in this book it is important to start off with a clear bright energy – this simple activation technique is a great way to begin any exercises where you are connecting to spirit.

Step 1. Rainbow Cleanse: Imagine breathing in rainbow colours into your body and out into the space around you. This will cleanse your energy field.

Step 2. Beam of Light: Imagine a White pillar of light from way above your head, moving down through your body like a big beam of light into the earth below you. Continue bringing this pillar of light down into the earth, allow this cycle of healing, grounding and rejuvenating light to enlarge and enhance your aura and energy field.

Step 3. Trance: Close your eyes and take several big belly breaths and slowly breathe. Relax your shoulders and body as you breathe in 4 counts, hold for 4 counts, breathe out for 4 counts and hold for 4. Repeat. Ask that all your chakras open up and spin well. 10 of these deep belly breath cycles will take you into a relaxing alpha/theta trance-like state.

(Please Refer to a more detailed version of this exercise in Chapter 1)

Step 4. Now, ask for your Spirit Guide/Higher self to assist you clearly and effectively. Call them in three times as this is known to be more powerful. It's like ringing up the Spirit hotline to help you! Now that you are tuned in, open up your "Clairs" and sense what you feel, sense, see, know, taste, smell around you!

Exercise: Animal Communication

Note: Animal communication can be used on pets who are living or have crossed over as everything is still energy! Pets are wonderful to communicate with. Animals have such a pure, lovely energy.

After completing the 4-step activation:

Say the animal/pet's name three times so you can merge and tune into it's energy.

Sense a colour or vibration around the pet and yourself.

Open your heart and smile, as this will help the animal align with your energy field. Relax and tap into your "clair" senses and notice visions, colours, words, smells, etc.

Say from your mind (telepathically) to their mind that you are grateful to connect with their spirit and energy and ask them some questions.

Keep practising and watch your ability to tune in grow over time as you develop your skills and your guides become used to working with your psychic and intuitive abilities.

Exercise: Magazine Channel

This exercise will help you to practise channelling information and how to write down the stream of insights that come through you.

Hold a magazine but do not open it.

Choose a page number e.g. 14. Tap into the pages energy BEFORE you open up to the page you have chosen. Do this by holding the magazine. Do 10 deep power breaths. Allow your chakras and clairs to open up. Write down what impressions you receive.

Open to the page and see what elements you intuitively got right and how certain ideas were communicated to you.

A friend did this and saw a magnifying glass and she thought it must be about glasses. Funnily enough she opened the magazine to the page she chose and there was a spectacles glasses advert on the page. Another friend saw the number 100 and, when she opened the page up she saw an advert selling an item for $100.

Challenge yourself and enjoy the process. You'll be amazed how the omniscient superconscious is always speaking to us!

CHAPTER 8

Auras & How to Read Them

Auras surround all living things on the planet. The aura is like an egg-shaped bubble of electromagnetic-energy which radiates out about 1 metre or so from our physical body. It is said the aura has 7 different layers that blend into each other. Our remarkable aura affects the way we feel, think and behave. It's part of who we are, part of our spirit. I hope in the future there is more research on the human aura so we can understand ourselves better.

We actually merge with other peoples auras as they expand out from our bodies. We may even say, "She has an aura about her," or "He seemed flat today." In fact all living things generate this field of energy. It's what makes us who we are. It's our life force, our energy system.

Many moons ago I attended an interesting Aura workshop. We all sat in a comfortable lounge room enthusiastically waiting to read auras. The room was semi-dark. The teacher picked someone to stand up against a wall while the rest of us de-focused and gazed at them. We relaxed our eyes and peered at the body's outline in an effort to detect the elusive aura. At best we saw a subtle outline or coloured glow, that appeared around the body. It was a challenge to see auras but sometimes a very thin line of green or blue would appear around the body especially the hands. Seeing auras like this is a good way to start but over time I developed my own way of reading auras that is more accurate. I teach students my style of how to read auras. Some students pick it up quickly while others need more time to develop the ability of seeing colours around the human body.

Melanie's Blue Aura

I did a spiritual talk at a local psychic fair one weekend. I asked for a volunteer to come up and get an aura and palm reading done. A sea of hands went up. I chose Melanie to come out the front.

She eagerly ran up to me at the front of the room. I took a breath, relaxed and opened my third eye to "see" her aura. I saw a hue of soft blue colour around her body. I told Melanie that blue represents spirituality.

People with blue auras usually love anything metaphysical. They also have compassionate hearts. I also saw a black and white dog in her aura. Melanie confirmed that she did have a dog like this. After the talk I went back to my stall and continued my readings and healings.

At the end of the day, Melanie rushed up to me at my stall. Melanie showed me a blue-aura photo, "You're so accurate! I just had my aura photo taken and it was blue!" she beamed.

I feel our aura changes depending on our feelings, thoughts and food we eat. Auras are influenced also by our exercise and how much we relax/meditate. Our bodies are dynamic energies of light that are constantly changing and flowing. Over the years my ability to see auras has strengthened. I feel meditation helps my chakras to open which allows me to see auras better. We are all born with amazing energy within and around us.

Sophia's Aura

Sophia came to me for a reading one day. I opened my third-eye vision and noticed that she had green, blue and purple colours in her aura. I tuned into the colours to see if I could tap into any vibrations or energetic messages that the colours held. For some reason, on this day, the colours seemed to be very alive and vibrant. The blue colour showed me an image of a baby in spirit. I asked Sophia if she had lost a baby. She cried and said she had terminated a baby 20 years ago. This baby in spirit began passing on beautiful messages to Sophia about her life. The session was very cathartic as Sophia had repressed grief that finally had a chance to express itself and be healed. Remember to open up and see what comes to you and to expect the unexpected!

Seeing Auras

Most clients are quite intrigued as to what their aura looks like. Some people have a mix of colours while others have predominately one colour. Some people may have colour on only certain parts of their body. People who are feeling sad or depressed may have an aura with grey colour in it. When I see a client I internally say to myself, "let me see their aura please." This allows a part of my mind to open up to view the client's aura.

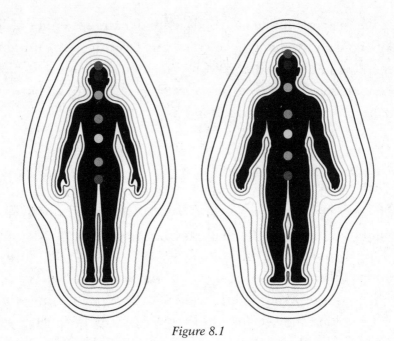

Figure 8.1

Aura Colours

Nicole's Red Hue

Nicole arrived for a reading one sunny day. I relaxed my eyes so I could tune into her aura. I noticed Nicole had a small red hue around her left shoulder. I merged with the red cloud and felt an uneasy feeling, almost painful and tender. "Do you have a sore shoulder?" I enquired. Nicole affirmed that her shoulder had been bothering her and that it was sore.

Red colour on some people may mean drive and passion. While on another person it may mean an ache as it did in the story above. It's best to tune into the colour and ask the colour what it means. Use your intuition to tap into the vibration and energy of the colours you view. When I teach courses students often ask me whether I see the colours physically around the person or, do I see the colour in my mind's eye. This is a great question. I do see soft colours around most people. Occasionally I see the aura colours in my mind's eye.

Some people tell me they don't see colours but they FEEL colours around people. Some people see colours in their mind's eye whereas others, like myself, see colours mostly around peoples bodies. I have a family member Tegan who sees colours around numbers and letters. Tegan is able to see words or numbers in her mind and can tell you the colours that are around them. Science calls this synesthesia.

"Synesthetic perceptions are specific to each person. Different people with synesthesia almost always disagree on their perceptions. In other words, if one synesthete thinks that the letter "q" is coloured blue, another synesthete might see "q" as orange."[14]

I love the way we humans are so unique in our intuitive abilities. Keep practising and asking your guides to show you people's auras as the more you practise the more this skill will develop.

Have a look at auras around crystals, animals, plants, trees, flowers or even vitamins. Our cat has a beautiful green aura although sometimes it has blue hues in it as well. When my cat is annoyed her aura has more brown tones in it.

Basic Colour Meanings Guide:

Here is a basic guideline of what some colours mean. Remember to always follow your own intuition.

Red

Represents action, passion, confidence, zest and power. Red is a dynamic colour but it also can mean a person needs to balance their energies. Person may also need some calming and tranquil energy to relax and recharge their nervous systems. It can mean inflammation in the body either physically or emotionally.

---

14 https://faculty.washington.edu/chudler/syne.html

Orange

This represents the sacral chakra. It's the colour of creativity and intimacy. People with an orange aura can be quite headstrong. They like a challenge and are go-getters. These people would benefit from meditation to harness this creative power and channel it in the right direction. I have seen a few people with apricot in their aura. When I tune into this colour it usually shows me the energy of compassion, an open heart and the willingness to forgive. People with orange hues in their aura are thoughtful and generous.

Yellow

Yellow in the aura represents intellect and the 3rd chakra which is the solar plexus. The yellow colour may reveal a childhood vision as this chakra holds memories. These people are intellectual and like to think. They may be overly critical. These people are fun, talkative and usually have a positive outlook on life. They are playful and love being in nature.

Green

A green aura usually symbolises healing. The person may be a natural healer. It may also mean a part of the person's body is being healed. People who have green auras are usually cheerful souls. They are usually empaths who feel other people's feelings. They need to have boundaries with themselves and to remember that they are not responsible for another person's emotions. When someone is upset it's best to send that person love. It's good to say a silent prayer (affirmation) and send positive intentions to that person. Sending love energy is a much better way to support someone and allows that person to walk their own karma and become empowered. People with green auras are intuitive. They may have strong gut feelings and this can come across sometimes as domineering. They may like gardening and have a "green thumb."

Blue

Blue auras are on people who are kind and giving. They sometimes give too much! They deserve self-love and need to nurture self as giving all the time may deplete their energy field. Many people I see with blue in their aura are spiritual people who are drawn towards psychic knowledge and the mystical side of life. People with blue auras are said to be natural counsellors and inspire others. They may find that people open up to them because of their warmth and friendliness.

Purple

Purple hues in the aura may appear as violet or lilac colours. A purple aura may indicate a person with a mission in life. These people are usually guided to doing what they need to along their path. It may be writing a book, teaching a course, volunteer work or supporting family members in their lives. They don't need accolades, they just like to flow along their life's journey. People with purple hues usually have good intentions and a good sense of humour. Listening to their own hearts allows violets to stay true to themselves and not to get caught up in life dramas. Violets may be ungrounded so they need to remember to connect with the earth and eat a balanced diet.

Pink

Pink-aura people are by nature loving and helpful. They are the nurturers who care for others. They are optimists who see the silver lining in all situations. Pink-aura people are romantic, faithful and loyal partners. They are creative and have good imaginations. They may enjoy writing poetry and song lyrics. They strive to make the world a better place. People with pink auras have good morals and values and enjoy being around animals.

Brown

Brown earthy colours in an aura mean a person likes connecting with the ground and is drawn to the earth. Sometimes a dark-brown aura can indicate confusion and unsettled energy. Person may need to have a good cleanse and to dig deep into their heart to find the peace they so deserve.

Grey

May indicate negative thoughts and thought forms. Also grey in the aura may represent fears and unresolved emotions. Person needs to face their feelings and to consider steps to take to resolve hidden issues. Healing is attainable.

Silver

I have seen a silver aura on only a few people. People with silver auras have a mission to help others. I saw a famous actor with a silver aura and through his fame he promotes positive causes to help the community. People with silver auras are deep, philosophical thinkers who like to look beneath the surface and to find out how to resolve issues. They have a deep drive to move forward with connection and devotion to self and others. They attract abundance into their lives.

Gold

Gold-coloured auras represent someone who is charismatic and a good listener. They also signify someone who has a purpose which drives them towards healing, support and fruitful outcomes. They think outside the box and see the big picture. They like to read about how Masters and Higher Beings impacted the earthly plane.

A Gold Aura

I was doing Platform Mediumship at a public Spritualty event to an audience of about 60 people. I stood up in front of everyone and held onto a microphone. I scanned the room and waited to see who I was drawn to read. I spotted a man sitting down the back of the room. "Can I come to you?" I asked. "Yes", he answered.

I moved closer to that area of the room. I took a deep breath and tuned in to the energy around his body.

I like to start reading the aura colours first as it helps me to tune into the person's energy field. Also looking at the aura first allows my third eye and, other senses, to tap into Spirit guides and family members who have crossed over.

I was surprised to see gold in this man's aura. What astounded me more was that I saw an image of Buddha floating in his energy field!

I proceeded to do a mini-reading on him. I told him he was in a helping profession and that I saw him speaking in front of a group of people. After the session this man approached me and said he was surprised with the information that I had shared. He informed me he was a paramedic. He said he trains people and that he was currently reading lots of information about Buddha.

Exercise: How to Read Auras

Remember that you may see the colours in your mind's eye or, around the person's body. The colours may look like patches, clouds or smudges.

Start With Anna's 4-Step Activation
1. *Rainbow Cleanse:* Imagine breathing in rainbow colours into your body and out into the space around you. This will cleanse your energy field.

2. *Beam of Light:* Imagine a White pillar of light from way above your head, moving down through your body like a big beam of light into the earth below you. Continue bringing this pillar of light down into the earth, allow this cycle of healing, grounding and rejuvenating light to enlarge and enhance your aura and energy field.

3. *Trance:* Close your eyes and take several big belly breaths and slowly breathe. Relax your shoulders and body as you breathe in 4 counts, hold for 4 counts, breathe out for 4 counts and hold for 4. Repeat. Ask that all your chakras open up and spin well. 10 of these deep belly breath cycles will take you into a relaxing alpha/theta trance-like state.

4. Now, ask for your Spirit Guide/Higher self to assist you clearly and effectively. Call them in three times as this is known to be more powerful. It's like ringing up the Spirit hotline to help you!

Now that you are tuned in Open up your "Clairs" and sense what you feel, sense, see, know, taste, smell around you!

To Start Reading Auras

Begin by practising on your own human hand. Look at your hand and blur your eyes.

Ask and have the intention that you want to see the aura. Tune into the energy of the hand and ask its vibration to communicate energetically with you. What do you see? Merge with what you notice. What feelings, insight, wisdom do you receive?

Now look at the auras of a pet, plant, tree or person. Even try looking at pictures as this will work too.

Keep on practising your psychic muscle so your skills will grow and expand!

CHAPTER 9

Scrying, Psychometry & Tea Leaf Reading

"The world is what you think it is."[15]

Psychometry is the art of holding an object to gain psychic impressions. By holding someone's hand, jewellery, letter or photo a person is able to receive insights into another person's energy. These psychic insights may come to you via visions, sounds, images, knowingness or feelings. Psychometry is also a type of scrying.

I first learned psychometry at a psychic workshop. I remember holding a silver watch which belonged to another participant whose name was Laura. I closed my eyes to tap into the energy emanating from her watch and immediately got the image of a young boy, water and overseas travel.

"Yes, I have a son who is travelling overseas to New Zealand to see his friend." Laura replied surprised and delighted. It was great to get

---

15 Dale, C. (2013) *The Subtle Body Practice manual*, Sounds True, USA.

feedback from Laura. It made me realise the power of psychometry and how energy can be read. This workshop made me eager to explore more about the art of psychometry and the psychic world.

Some psychics will hold onto a person's hand as a way of connecting to the person's spirit and energy. Other psychics just sit close by to tune into the energy of the client. Some psychics like to look at pictures and encourage clients to bring photos along to their sessions. My client Teresa lost her son Marc in a motorbike accident. Teresa brought along Marc's favourite items and showed them to me. Through psychometry I was able to hold these items and tune into the energy and spirit of her son to pass on messages. At the end of the session Teresa could feel a feather-like touch on her cheek, "I now know he's around me and that gives me great comfort", she said.

Psychometry Exercises

I attended a spiritual group for a few years and the teacher would organise fun psychic activities. One evening we all put one item of jewellery onto a tray. The tray soon filled up with rings, bangles and watches. The tray was then passed around the room to each person. We randomly picked up somebody else's jewellery not knowing who owned it. We closed our eyes and held the item. I held onto a gold bangle with a lovely design on it. I like to write down my impressions so I scribbled some information on a piece of paper. It was like automatic writing. I wrote down images, words or feelings that came from the gold bangle. We then took turns to share our insights and only revealed who owned an item when everyone was finished sharing.

Exercise A – Known Item

One of the best ways to practice intuition is to sometimes practice on things you know the answers to. This is because it will help you to learn about how your intuition works. Begin by holding a piece of your jewellery or an item of your clothing.

1. Pick up an item that you own.

2. Close your eyes and tune into that item.

3. Breathe deeply, relax and allow insights to come to you.

4. Ask the item's energy to communicate to you.

5. Ask questions and be open to receiving images, feelings, sensations.

6. Ask about the past, present and future. Right down any impressions, feelings, symbols or words that you receive.

7. Good luck. Practise on family and friends. Get their permission first.

Exercise B – Who are they?

1. Open up a newspaper or magazine article. You could do this online as well.

2. Flick though the magazine and find an article on someone you don't know. Do not read the article. Cover up the words. Look at the picture only.

3. Tune into the picture. Merge with the energy of the person/s in the picture.

4. Intuitively find out what's happened in that person's life. As you connect with their energy you may like to imagine you're looking at a movie screen in your mind. What images are appearing to you? Open up all your senses and chakras.

5. Call in your higher self and guides, ask about the person's past, present and future.

Some people do this type of exercise using pictures of famous people. Be creative and have fun!

Exercise C – Flower

Flowers are great to read as they are living things just like us. Flowers grow and die; they produce young; they are made of cells; they need energy, nutrients, air and water to survive; they react to the environment around them.

1. Gather a group of friends and do flower readings on each other.
2. Do not let each other see the flower you are holding.
3. At the end choose another person's flower to tune into and read the energy of the flower. The flower's vibrational energy will share information with you.

You can also go into your garden and choose a flower or leaf, hold onto it, and see what messages nature has for you.

Exercise D – Jewellery and Crystals

A great activity to do with a psychic group is to have everyone put one item of jewellery onto a tray.

1. Everyone randomly picks a piece of jewellery from the tray and does an impromptu reading.
2. Hold the item and note down any impressions you get from it, similar to automatic writing.
3. Once everyone is finished, take turns to share your impressions.
4. Only reveal the owner of the jewellery once everyone has had a turn.

It's also interesting to do this activity with crystals.

1. Everyone in the group holds a different crystal for a few minutes so their energy can be absorbed by the crystal.

2. Now place the crystals into a bowl.

3. The bowl is then passed around and people collect a random crystal and read the crystal.

It's amazing what people pick up from tapping into the energy of the crystal. I enjoy doing these activities when I teach my courses.

How to Scry:

Scrying is a technique where you stare or gaze into something such as water, metal or smoke. Scrying is also called crystal gazing. I like to use scrying when I am doing palmistry or giving psychic readings. Scrying allows me to tap into the energy of the person and gives me information that's pertinent to them.

I learnt scrying many years ago at a psychic class that I attended. One night the teacher placed several crystal balls around the room. She told us we were going to learn how to scry. The teacher took us into a deep meditation to prepare us for the scrying activity. I held a beautiful amethyst crystal ball and peered into it. As I looked into the crystal ball I saw a forest with galloping horses running amongst the trees. The vision appeared to me very quickly. It was exciting to see how scrying worked.

The teacher also showed us how to scry using a mirror or a door. I have since learnt that scrying can be done on many things. Just breathe deeply and relax, look at something, defocus your eyes, and scry! Some people scry with open eyes while others scry with their closed eyes. A student in my Psychic Toolbox class asked me if images come into my mind's eye (inside the head) or are images seen around them. I replied that some people are stronger in one method or the other. See which works best for you.

Exercise 1: Green Apple

1. Imagine a green apple with a smiley face on it.

2. Where do you 'see' that image? Is the green apple suspended in space in front of you or, inside your head/third eye area?

3. Maybe you do not see a picture but you sense it in some other way.

4. Take note and practise more.

5. Now, imagine a bowl of fruit.

6. Where does the image appear to you?

7. Imagine yourself opening the door to your house. Walk inside your house, go to the kitchen and get a glass of water.

8. Find somewhere to sit. Where are all the images appearing to you?

9. Repeat it and notice clearly what's happening with these thoughts.

Be aware of your senses and how your mind forms these images for you. Journal your experiences if you wish and see if they change over time.

Exercise 2: Preparing to Scry

Note: Begin with the **4-Step Activation Sequence** to help you tune in and shift your brain-wave energy and vibration.

1. *Rainbow Cleanse:* Imagine breathing in rainbow colours into your body and out into the space around you. This will cleanse your energy field.

2. *Beam of Light:* Imagine a White pillar of light from way above your head, moving down through your body like a big beam of light into the earth below you. Continue bringing this pillar of light down into the earth, allow this cycle of healing, grounding and rejuvenating light to enlarge and enhance your aura and energy field.

3. *Trance:* Close your eyes and take several big belly breaths and slowly breathe. Relax your shoulders and body as you breathe in 4 counts, hold for 4 counts, breathe out for 4 counts and hold for 4. Repeat. Ask that all your chakras open up and spin well. 10 of these deep belly breath cycles will take you into a relaxing alpha/theta trance-like state.

(Please Refer to a more detailed version of this exercise in Chapter 1)

4. Now, ask for your Spirit Guide/Higher self to assist you clearly and effectively. Call them in three times as this is known to be more powerful. It's like ringing up the Spirit hotline to help you! Now that you are tuned in Open up your "Clairs" and sense what you feel, sense, see, know, taste, smell around you!

Exercise 3: Hand Scry

1. Look at both of your palms, connect with their energy by blurring your eyes and seeing if any colours, images, scenes, words or feelings appear to you.

2. Ask your hands what message they have for you. You may be surprised by what you find! Allow your intuition and Guide to help you. Relax and allow it to come to you. The more you breathe deeply and relax beforehand, the more you will get info, as your brain will be in an alpha/theta state where the subconscious and superconscious realms are.

3. Turn your hands over and look at the back of them and feel their energy. What do you see/sense? Turn them over again and ask divine wisdom for more information about your hands. Tune into the centre part of the palm and ask the Higher Self to give you any messages and feel the energy from that centre part of the palm.

4. Repeat these steps as the more you practise the more you will be able to tune in better.

Advance Tip: Scrying can be done using a piece of paper, a door or any surface or area.

Try scrying a flower or an animal. Feel the energy and presence that emanates from them. Do they have a message for you? Merge with their energy and tune into the vibrations.

Tea Leaf Reading

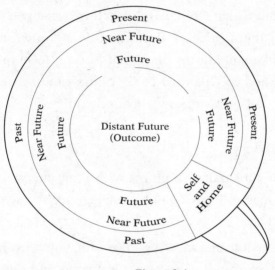

Figure 9.1

Tea leaf reading is an ancient practice. It is a tool for tapping into the subconscious and superconscious by looking at the patterns and shapes in the tea leaves. Reading the Tea Leaves (or coffee grounds) is also a form of scrying. Tea leaf reading is easy, fun and enlightening! Tea leaf reading is also called tasseomancy or tassology. Coffee reading is known as cafeomancy. Tasseography and cafeomancy are also meditative tools which provide deep insights.

Tea leaf reading is a joyful, intuitive and creative way to listen and tune into yourself, and others who come to you for a reading. You can also read for yourself which is a great way to tap into another realm.

How to do Tea Leaf Reading

Step 1: Have a cup of tea

Make a cup of tea from loose tea leaves. You can use teabags too. Herbal teas work well too. Use coffee grounds if you wish to instead of tea.

Step 2: Drink your tea

Drink your tea, but remember to leave some liquid at the bottom of the cup or mug. As you sip your tea quiet your mind and relax. Take time to drink your tea in a relaxed, present way. Notice how you are breathing and the taste of the tea. As you breathe deeply allow yourself to go into a still and calm place. Reading the tea leaves patterns and symbols takes concentration and intuition so the more you are relaxed the better you can tune in.

Step 3: At the Bottom of the Cup

Leave a small amount of tea liquid at the bottom of your cup. Leaving about 1–2 teaspoons of liquid at the bottom of the cup is ideal. (If you are using a teabag open it up and allow some of the tea leaves to fall into the small amount of tea water at the bottom of your cup.)

Step 4: Swirl three times

Hold your, almost empty, teacup in your hand. Swirl it around 3 times clockwise. The tea leaves will spread gently around the inside of the cup. Now turn your teacup over onto a saucer (or plate). Rotate it 3 times in an anticlockwise direction. The remaining liquid is now on the saucer yet some of the leaves will remain on the interior of the cup for you to read. Breathe 3 times before you turn the cup over and then begin to read the tea leaves!

Note: some psychics read the saucers as well.

Step 5: Patterns and symbols

Identify the patterns and symbols and write them down.

Tea leaf reading is an art form. Different people will perceive different images depending on their own experiences and the insight that comes through them.

If your cup has a handle, start from there. Read clockwise, from the handle, around the cup. If your cup has no handle, begin reading from 12 o'clock at the top of the cup or, wherever you intuitively feel you would like to start from. Take note of the first symbol you see as this will set the scene for the whole reading. Divide the cup into three sections: rim(top), middle and bottom/base. Take your time and focus on what thoughts, feelings and visions you gain from peering into the wonders of the tea cup and its leaves.

Step 6: Create your tea leaf reading

You may like to write down what symbols you see. Record intuitively what the symbols or patterns mean to you. You may prefer to just speak and allow yourself to channel any information that you may want to share.

Allow the symbols and patterns you see to tell you a story. Provide the information you have to the sitter in a loving, kind way. If you are giving the reading you may be called the seer.

Symbol Interpretations

You can use your own intuition, or a dream dictionary, to help you decipher the symbols and patterns you may find.

Different people may interpret the same symbol differently. For example; a plane to one person may intuitively mean an upcoming trip while to another it may mean flying high and succeeding in a current project.

AIRCRAFT – journey; travel

ALLIGATOR or CROCODILE – beware and protect yourself, have boundaries

ANCHOR – get some stability in your life

ANGEL – good news coming, help is with you

ANT – busy time for you

APPLE – achievement and abundance

ARCH – opportunity coming

ARROW – up = good direction, down = reconsider

BABY – new life

BIRD – new direction

BOUQUET – love ; validation for your efforts

BALLOON – fun, social life

BASKET – harvest, abundance

BED – sleep on it before making a decision or, rest more

BEE – fruitful rewarding work

BELL – good news; call to attention

BICYCLE – balance

BIRD – good news or message coming soon

BOAT – worthwhile journey/event

BOWL – invitations, money or generosity

BUBBLES – floating on the cup of tea, or coffee, means money coming in

BUGS – distractions; need for focus

BUTTERFLY – joy is coming to you

CAKE – birthday or celebration

CAMEL – sustenance and energy

CANDLE – you will be shown the way ahead. Watch for signs in dreams, songs, etc.

CHAIR – a guest is coming

CLOCK – don't waste time, get to it!

COIN – money coming your way

COMB – how is your self-worth? Give yourself some self-love

DASHES or DOTS – short trips/events ahead

DOG – a good friend

DOOR – opportunities ahead for you to walk through

DRUM – a change, take action

EAR – listen and reflect

EGG – new beginnings

ELEPHANT – be patient, support will come

ENVELOPE – a message for you

EXCLAMATION MARK – pay attention!

FENCE – limits and boundaries

FLOWER – praise and gratitude

FLY – annoyances or, move quickly

FOOT – which direction are you going?

FORK – decision time; fork in the road

FRUIT – prosperity and fun

FROG – fertility; abundance

GATE – new prospects around you

HAMMER – get your point across

HARP – love and romance

HAT – a change in roles will benefit you; wearing many hats

HILLS – challenges you will overcome

HORSESHOE – good luck

JEWELS – you are valuable

KANGAROO – leaping ahead

KETTLE – a special visitor will come your way

KITE – your wish will be granted

KNIFE – watch what you say and how you communicate

LADDER – going up in life, improving

LEAF – turning over of a new leaf; you're ready for it!

LIGHTENING – sudden insights will be fabulous for you

LINES – journey towards your life path

LION – an influential contact

MASK – a secret to be kept

MOUNTAIN – a goal

NEEDLE – a healing or repair

PALM TREE – holiday, relax

QUESTION MARK – rethink your plans

RABBIT – fertility in family or business

RAINBOW – good fortune ahead

RING – success, completion

ROSE – romance; love given

SCISSORS – remove yourself if need be and change your perception

SHEEP – a calm and peaceful person

SHELL – you will find a simple treasure

SNAKE – transformation and healing

SPIDER – what are you weaving/creating?

SPOON – generosity

STAR – success & achievement

STAIRS – things will improve

SUN – accomplishment

TENT – camping or, something hidden

TURTLE – take your time, rewards will come

TRIANGLE – positive change

UMBRELLA – protect yourself

VASE – a friend may need some advice

VOLCANO – release your emotions wisely, see a counsellor if need be

WASP – issues need resolving

CHAPTER 10

Tarot & Oracle Cards

"How people treat you is their karma. How you react is yours."

Wayne Dyer[16]

Tarot and Oracle cards are a wonderful tool to use when reading for yourself and others. There are so many decks of oracle or tarot cards to purchase. I have quite a few decks of cards. I like having a variety to choose from, but sometimes I buy a set of cards that I do not need so I give them away or sell second-hand. The cards usually have a booklet that comes with them which explains layouts and card meanings.

The Cards

Oracle cards have about 44–55 cards per deck. Many oracle card decks have interesting pictures and are enlightening to use. Tarot card packs have 78 cards in them and are linked back in history to China, India and Egypt. Tarot cards are divided into major and minor cards.

---

16 Van Praggh. J. (2014) *Adventures of the Soul* (p.90), Hay House, US.

It's fun to do one of the simple card spreads from the card booklets or you can design your own card layout. I have tried many card layouts over the years, but the most common card layout I use is the three-card spread which simply reads as past, present and future.

Cleansing the Cards

Some people blow gently on the cards to clear the energy. Others knock their knuckles or tap on the cards. I find shuffling is also an effective way to clear the energy and gain guidance from the cards. You can also place a crystal on top of your deck, to cleanse and revitalise the cards energy.

Using the Cards

When you read for yourself, shuffle the cards and ask a question. You can also ask the universe to help you in learning more about something that's happening in your life. Place a few cards in front you and get a feel for what the cards are trying to convey to you.

I enjoy using tarot and oracle cards in my reading sessions. I also like to add palmistry and aura/chakra readings. I also love to have clients choose a free card to take home. The free cards come from inspirational card packs that I have purchased. It also amazes me that the card the client randomly chooses relates to what is happening in their current life and what was discussed in their reading.

Several years ago I was working at a psychic fair doing back-to-back readings. A young man sat in front of me and asked about his business prospects. He said that he had been an alcoholic and had stopped drinking so that he could get his life together. I was surprised when I saw in my mind's eye an image of the Empress tarot card. The Empress card in the original Rider Waite tarot is one of abundance. I took a deep breath as I tuned into the energy of what the Empress card wanted to share to this young man. The Empress card shared its message and the young man received insight as to what would help him reach his goals.

In my twenties, I was taught how to read the Rider Waite Tarot deck by a local psychic called Paulo. In my Tarot lessons Paulo would walk me through the symbology and meaning of the images on the cards. Afterwards I would excitedly go home to study the cards meanings. Over the years I have practised many different tarot layouts in the hope of finding answers and gain insight. I still refer to the Rider Waite cards although I do like to use other decks too. When I travel I like to pack card decks. Some of my clients use card deck apps on their phones.

The tarot, like any psychic tool, can be used to help tune into your past, present and future. But nothing is set in stone. Psychic information can change depending on people's choices and decisions they make. A tarot reader may see you with three children in the future, but the final choice is always yours. You can change predictions depending on your goals and aims in life. The future is in your hands!

Nathan's Insight

Nathan, aged 33, came back for another reading. He sat at my reading table which was adorned with tarot cards, crystals and a lit candle.

Nathan had a depth of understanding about spirituality which I found quite refreshing. He was also aware that this wisdom had come from the pain and challenges in his life.

"You know Anna" he explained, "Spirit does not always give us all the answers and they like us to work it out for ourselves sometimes." I smiled and nodded. I wholeheartedly agreed with Nathan.

Good psychics are amazing spiritual counsellors that help you tap into your own intuition and inner guidance. But they won't have all the answers for you. The spirit world wants us to use our own free will to make decisions. Every decision we make is made from the level of consciousness we have at the time. The choices I made in my 20s are different to the ones I would now make in my 50s, as my understanding about myself, others and life has changed so much. Spirit wants us to create our own path.

It is said that this earth plane is like a school. We are given tests that we need to pass before we move onto the next level. When we are challenged, it gives us the opportunity to use our heart to solve the challenge. To love the unlovable is a big test for many humans.

There is so much grace, serenity and magic in this world. I had a friend who was annoyed she didn't get the job she wanted. But not long after life offered her an even better opportunity. If one door closes it's because another, better door is waiting to open for you! Let Go and Believe that Life has your best interest at heart.

Choosing a Deck

My mum works at a local charity shop. A few years ago mum gave me a tarot set she picked up from the second-hand shop. The near new tarot cards were beautifully placed in a stunning box and were wrapped in a shiny purple cloth. I tried hard to love the deck, but we never really bonded. The images on the cards were unusual and I found it a challenge to tune into the pictures. I ended up giving them to a friend who had showed interest in them.

Choose a deck you feel drawn to so you can develop a relationship with their energy, character and beauty. Starting with a traditional pack, while you are learning, is a good idea as they were designed with specific symbolism which can help you learn faster. As you develop, pick out a deck which suits your character and energy. The right deck will speak to you and you'll know they are right for you.

Choosing a Card Spread

Most tarot/oracle decks include a booklet with a few layouts and spreads in it. You can also design your own spread. This can be fun to do. The cards have an energy of their own and they will work with you to help your heart's desire and wishes.

The best way to learn is to start with simple readings like the three-card spread which lays out one card for past, then a card for present and a final card for future.

Practice readings on yourself and a friend, or family member. Reading the tarot and oracle cards is like learning a new language. Learn the cards and their symbology so then you can string together the meaning that they have in a spread.

The more you practise the more you can connect with how the pack communicates with you. I still love learning new things about tarot/ oracle cards and I adore teaching tarot classes. Below are a couple of great spreads I designed to use with clients.

Anna's Cosmic Wheel Spread

Place 12 cards in a circle pattern.

1. Begin at number 1 and go around the circle until the last card is in area 12.

(You can put down an extra card over each number to gain more messages and guidance.)

2. Each area, or house, holds information about the person's life. Tune into the vibration of the cosmic houses and allow the vibration of the house to tell you more about the person you are reading for.

3. Do a reading on yourself and see the amazing messages the Cosmic Wheel has for you!

4. This Cosmic Wheel Spread is based on Astrology Houses.

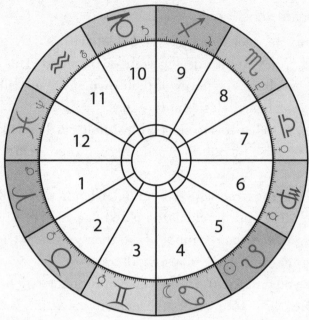

Figure 10.1

1. My Self: Identity, appearance, vitality, past lives, inner passions, self-awareness, outlook, blocks and Gifts.

2. My Worth: Self-worth, abundance, money, routines, wealth, responsibility, self-esteem, security, values.

3. My Expression: Communication, speak, write, media, siblings, community and school.

4. My Home: Family, emotions, parents, ancestors, traditions, subconscious patterns.

5. My Activity: Play, creativity, children, romance, intimacy, entertainment, hobbies.

6. My Health: Nutrition, fitness, exercise, self-improvement, pets.

7. My Unions: Relationships, love, companions, sharing, legal, business partnerships.

8. My Drive: Rebirth, renewal, shared money and property, inheritance, sex.

9. My Expansion: Travel, study, higher learning, ethics, faith, dreams.

10. My Career: Goals, success, image, achievement.

11. My Networks: Friends, society, service, humanitarian, good luck.

12. My Soul: Spirituality, karma, evolution of the soul, coaching, healing, reflection.

13. Overall Vibration Card

14. The Higher Message For You is … Share your Insights.

Anna's Divine 10 Spread

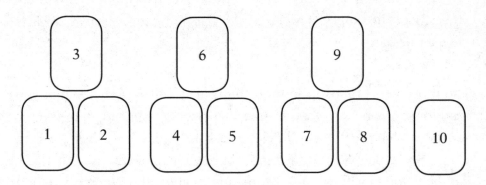

Figure 10.2

Cards 1, 2 = Past

Card 3 = Message For You is...

Cards 4, 5 = Present

Card 6 = Message For You is...

Cards 7, 8 = Future

Card 9 Message For You is...

Card 10 Overall Vibration Card

Alison's Flower

School teacher Alison arrived for a reading. I did a past, present and future reading for her using the Fairy tarot deck. I shuffled the cards and Alison picked some cards and placed them down on the table in front of her.

One card had pictures of flowers, garden and fairies on it. To my surprise one of the white flowers seemed to float up off the card. I paused in amazement and all of a sudden this knowingness (claircognizance) came over me.

"I feel there is a gardening event that you did well in organising. You will get rewarded for your efforts."

Alison looked surprised and said that she had built a garden at the school she taught at and that she was going to receive an award for her design.

The more you practise the more natural it will become. When you read for someone else you become a storyteller using all your psychic senses, and channelling abilities, to pass through what is best for your client. Some people study the tarot purely for personal use. The tarot can help you clarify what is happening in your life. When my daughter needs guidance in her life we will do a reading for her using a mix of tarot and oracle cards. She loves it and it gives her a chance to tune into the cards and read the messages from the booklet. This also helps her to tap into her own intuition and natural instincts.

Passing on Messages

Some psychic readers tell clients inappropriate things that may be damaging and hurtful. If a psychic tells someone that they see no future in someone's current relationship, the client may be left feeling lost, confused and with little hope for the future. I have seen happily married people who were upset by a reader's abrupt comments.

Just one unnecessary comment can cause chaos in someone's life. Be mindful and compassionate about what you say to someone. It is better not to make concrete predictions but rather pass through messages from spirit that will suggest what the energy of the relationship or situation is and what guidance the couple needs to take. Then leave it up to the client to follow through any suggestions that spirit has passed on.

Be aware of people's mental health, as some people can hide how fragile they may be feeling. Relationships are very complex and they can change quite quickly. Sometimes we are not told the full story about someone's relationship. Share loving comments from the spirit world. Pray and ask, after you have given a reading, that your client will be guided by divine spirit energy. Help the client to leave your session feeling empowered. Give them divine knowledge to help their relationship and, most importantly, their relationship with themselves as all relationships stem from the one we have with ourselves. It's important to also refer clients onto health professionals such as counsellors or psychologists if you feel they need these extra resources.

Adam & Elle

Adam was a 25-year-old male. He came along for a reading to ask me about whether he and his girlfriend Elle would last. Adam was thinking of marrying Elle.

I used the cards, along with my intuition, to tune into their relationship. I saw a vision of Adam and Elle showing their communication was poor and that there was a lot of anger between them. I also saw that they needed help to communicate and I suggested they seek out counselling so they could both learn better communication skills.

Spirit also took me back to his last relationship and how his last girlfriend had betrayed him. Adam realised his previous girlfriend had an effect on his current relationship. He was reflective about what came up in our session and left with more knowledge about steps to take in his future.

The tarot can help us to know ourselves better and to understand why things happen to us.

Many tarot readers use their intuition as well as the card pictures and vibrations to help them read for self or others.

Jumping cards jump out while you are shuffling the cards. Some people just put the jumping card back in the pack but often it has jumped out as it wants your attention. If a card has mysteriously been flicked out of the pack, take note of this card and tune into it as it has grabbed your attention for a reason. Some of the cards that have jumped out seem to do a mid-air dance that only a playful spirit would do!

Exercise: Tarot/ Oracle Card Reading

You will need a deck of Tarot or Oracle cards. Have a notebook and pen nearby.

1. Relax and begin by taking slow, deep breaths in through the nose (if possible) and out through the mouth. With each deep breath feel more and more relaxed.

2. Tap your cards. Imagine that this deck is surrounded by beautiful cleansing and healing light that will support you in this reading. Call in three times, your devoted guide and the wisdom of the cosmos.

3. As you hold your cards, ask a question in your mind or, out loud. For example, *"what do I need to know right now?"* or *"What messages do you have for me today?"*, *"How do I heal my relationship?"*

4. Trust that your guide is with you and will help you know the answers to your questions with the help of the cards.

5. Lay out the cards. Some people shuffle then choose cards from the top but you can also choose cards randomly from anywhere in the

deck. Sometimes I fan out the deck and ask the clients to choose a certain number of cards.

6. Have telepathic communication with the cards. They hold energy and you have sent them light (in step 2) so know that you have the energy of spirit in them to assist you find the wisdom and insight you desire.

7. Share your interpretation with an open heart. Spirit would not want you or your client to feel negative or hopeless, so share information that is uplifting, useful and inspiring.

8. At the end of the tarot/oracle reading thank the deck and the Higher Energies for their support and guidance.

Tarot Cards

The 78 cards in a tarot deck are divided into 22 cards called Major Arcana. The other 56 cards are called the Minor Arcana. The Minor Arcana are made up of four suits with each suit numbered 1(Ace) to 10.

The four suits are:

Wands represent action, spirit & fire

Cups represent our emotions/water

Swords represent the mind/air

Pentacles represent physical world/earth.

Also there are 4 court cards in each suit. They are called Page, Knight, Queen, King. You will find some tarot decks change the names of their cards.

The Rider Waite Tarot deck was developed in 1910 by A. E. Waite. The Rider Waite pictures were illustrated by artist Pamela Colman Smith. The Rider Waite Tarot deck format is copied by many tarot decks today. The original Rider Waite deck is a very good learning tool that has helped me understand tarot. You may find other tarot decks that you enjoy too.

TAROT

Table 10.1 Major Arcana:

0. Fool (Carefree)	6. Lovers (Connection)	11. Justice (Fair)	16. Tower (Restructure)
1. Magician (Action)	7. Chariot (Progress)	12. Hanged Man (Surrender)	17. Star (Positive)
2. High Priestess (Intuition)	8. Strength (Power)	13. Death (Transition)	18. Moon (Unsure)
3. Empress (Heart)	9. Hermit (Contemplate)	14. Temperance (Balance)	19. Sun (Success)
4. Emperor (Resilience)	10. Wheel of Fortune (Cycle of Life)	15. Devil (Fear)	20. Judgement (Choice)
5.Hierophant (Belief)			21. World (Completion)

Table 10.2 Tarot Four Suits:

SUIT	CARD	ELEMENT	MEANING
Swords	Spades	Air	Mind, Thoughts
Wands (or staves)	Clubs	Fire	Motivation, Creativity
Cups	Hearts	Water	Emotions, Love
Coins (or pentacles)	Diamonds	Earth	Possessions, Physical world

Table 10.3 Minor Arcana:

	Swords	Wands	Cups	Pentacles
ACE (1)	Power	Create	Triumph	Prosper
2	Choice	Plan	United	Balance
3	Nurture	Ideas	Celebration	Teamwork
4	Reflect	Harmony	Revise	Stability
5	Communication	Organise	Time out	Meditation
6	Transition	Victory	Happiness	Giving
7	Attitude	Challenge	Choice	Resources
8	Wait	Change	Quest	Achieving
9	Faith	Accomplish	Success	Gratitude
10	Rebirth	Slow down	Fulfilment	Abundance
Page	Perception	Ideas	Intuition	Manifest
Knight	Imagination	Vitality	Awareness	Focus
Queen	Vision	Passion	Compassion	Effort
King	Clarity	Motivation	Instinct	Action

Major Arcana

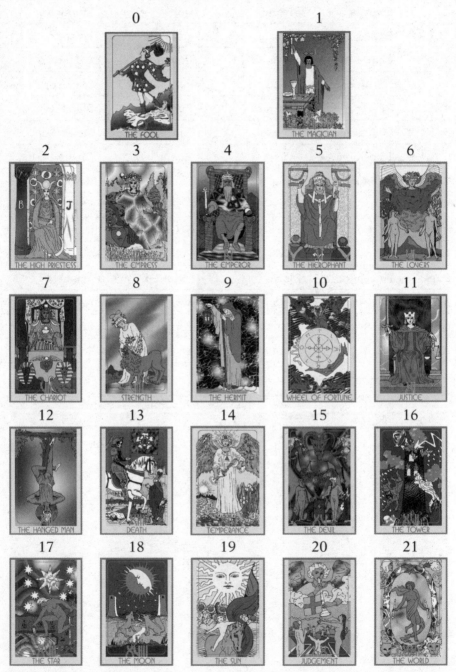

Colman-Smith Tarot Card Deck

Minor Arcana

Cups

Colman-Smith Tarot Card Deck

Minor Arcana

Pentacles

Colman-Smith Tarot Card Deck

Minor Arcana

Swords

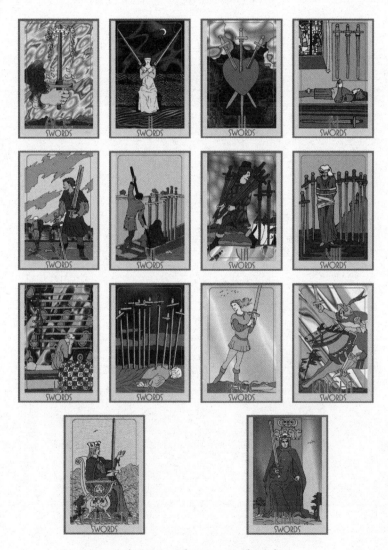

Colman-Smith Tarot Card Deck

Minor Arcana

Wands

Colman-Smith Tarot Card Deck

CHAPTER 11

Numerology Insights

"All power comes from within."[17]

Numerology is the ancient art of information based on the numbers connected to an individual. Numerology is based on the teachings of Pythagoras, a Greek mathematician, numerologist and astrologer born in 570 BC. Pythagoras believed that life revolved around cycles just like the orbits and cycles of the planets. According to Pythagoras, the entire destiny of a person could be decided primarily from the numbers involved in their date of birth and name.

9-Year Cycles

I use numerology to help a person see why certain events are happening in their lives. By looking at the endings and beginnings in someone's life we can get insight into the cycles that are running through a person's life.

---

17 Dale, C. (2013) *The Subtle Body Practice manual*, Sounds True, USA.

Numerology primarily uses the 9-year cycle as the base to deter-mine meanings and where people are in their life cycle.

Sometimes, even before I add up the numbers, it's easy to see where a person is in their 9-year cycle just by the events that are going on in their lives. Trisha came to me for a reading about her life. She had left a relationship and had taken time to heal her heart and discover new hobbies and passions. Trisha was ready now to embark on a new relationship and had tried internet dating. I felt Trisha was at the beginning of a 9-year cycle as she had let go of the past and was embracing new activities. I checked her birthdate to discover where she was in her 9-year cycle. Trisha was in the 1st year of her 9-year cycle. I worked this out by:

Current 9-year cycle is calculated by:

Examples:

Trisha was Born on 7th of April

The year we were in, at time of reading, was 2015

Add day of birth + month of birth + year you are currently in.

For example, Trisha's 9-Year Cycle Number is: 1

7 (day of her birth) + 4 (April is the 4th month) + 8 (2015 adds up to an 8 i.e. 2+0+1=5 = 8)

So this gives us the 7 + 4 + 8= 19 (1+9) = 1

Jared saw me for a reading. He was frustrated with his life and was looking for change in his career and love. He was born on 14th November and the reading was in 2016.

14 + 11+ 2016

5 (1 +4) + 2 (1 +1) + 9 =16 (1+6) = 7

Jared landed in a 7-year cycle. The wheels of change would turn as he headed towards the end of this 9-year cycle and started a new 9-year cycle. Changes can occur anywhere in a 9-year cycle but you will find big things happen at the beginning and end of cycles. There are great learnings, healings and growth to be gained from each cycle and that is the gift of being on this planet.

Sometimes our life works out differently than what we would like. There is a greater plan in place and it will guide you to what's most purposeful for you to gain the knowledge, insights and peace that your Spirit needs in this lifetime. The universe hears your thoughts and helps you to create a life that can expand and heal you. When a relationship ends, it's because it's time to learn more. When a career starts to turn sour it's because life is pushing you into something different. A new birth is being created for you. The key is not to make changes when they are not necessary. If things are working well in one area of your life be grateful and use your energy to work on another area and set new goals. Being grounded is important. If we are always complaining that life is not serving us it's usually because we aren't serving ourselves.

Number Meanings

Number 1 – represents FOCUS: Stay focused and aligned with your goals. Remember what you think is what you get so, are your thoughts in alignment with your goals?

Number 2 – represents LOVE: Continue to love self and others. You have learned some great lessons in your life. Embed these learnings into your life and know it is safe to love. Commit to opening your heart to love.

Number 3 – represents PEACE: You can create peace with your thoughts. Feed your mind loving with supportive self-talk.

Number 4 – represents BALANCE: Stay balanced in mind, body and spirit. A table needs four legs to stay balanced. Continue to strive to balance sleep, work, food and playtime!

Number 5 – represents CHANGE: You are a mirror of your life. Change is inevitable and comes to you when your Soul is ready. Embrace the changes and know that if one door closes another opens.

Number 6 – represents WISDOM: The greatest journey is from our head to our heart. As you travel through life you will gather friends but most of all you will befriend that beautiful Soul that YOU are. Wisdom is life's Gift to you.

Number 7 – represents REFLECTION: Your consciousness (thoughts) magnetises to you what's in your world. Visualise your aims and goals and see how these manifest in your life.

Number 8 – represents ABUNDANCE: You are worthy of life's greatest gifts. You are a magical and abundant Spirit. Enjoy accumulating a bounty of love, joy and peace on this planet.

Number 9 – represents SHIFTS: Profound shifts coming your way. Let go of what no longer serves you to make way for new growth. Just like a tree loses its leaves so it can have new growth. Do small things each day to support your changes. It will be SO worth it!

Number Sequences

Keep an eye out for any number sequences which occur during your day, particularly any repeating sequences such as phone numbers, licence plates or even clock times. The Universe is one big oracle card so these sequences are really just the universe sending messages to you.

I love when I see number sequences or letter combinations, especially on number plates. When I drove to Sydney to teach a course, I could predict how the weekend was going to go as I took note of the letter and number combinations. The world around you is always vibrating and it taps into your own magnetic vibration.

Are you listening to the universe communicating with you? My tip when reading number plates is to allow them to find you. You do not need to hunt for the messages, they will naturally occur when the time is right! I have also noticed birds that fly near your car, as you drive, are also signs from Spirit and Nature. Take note of whether the birds are flying towards your car (new information is coming to you) or birds flying in a forward direction (means heading in the right direction & new plan ahead).

Number Surprise

Numbers can pop up anywhere so be alert to any surprise messages the universe may provide. One day I was walking along the road and my eye spotted a 10 cent coin in the grass. I picked it up and smiled knowing the number 10 creates 1 as 1+0= 1. I asked the coin and the energy of the number one on the coin to share what number 1 represented for me. Its vibration and energy flowed into my heart as I channelled: "you have come a long way Dear One. More new discoveries ahead for you. Keep focusing on your goals as they are in alignment with your Soul. We love you and stand by you."

Number Patterns

You may notice repetitive number patterns on clocks, your computer or a receipt you receive from the grocery store. Take note of these numbers and tune into what they represent for you. Double and triple numbers such as 111, 222 or 333 hold significance as, if they are the same number their frequency is higher and it represents a message from the universe. I was at the bank recently and I had a pile of coins I wanted transferred into notes. The bank teller went over to the coin machine and came back with $123.45. My jaw dropped. Everything is in perfect order. What a beautiful natural sequence!

Key Numbers

Soul Path Number:

This number represents the inner talents and abilities and the lessons to be learned. It is the sum of the date, month and year numbers in one's birth date.

Soul Path is just adding up the numbers of your birth date like these examples.

They say if you know basic maths you can do numerology!

The trick is to keep going until only one number is left!

1. Soul Path = Month + Day + Year
2. Soul Path = e.g. Birthdate August 12th, 1978
   12 + 8 + 1978
3. Soul Path = (1 + 2) + (8) + (1 + 9 + 7 + 8)
4. Soul Path = 3 + 8 + 25
5. Soul Path = 3 + 8 + (2+ 5)
6. Soul Path = 3 + 8 + 7
7. Soul Path = 18
8. Soul Path = (1 + 8)
9. Soul Path = 9

Soul Path Examples

1. Jessica's Birthdate is 05.12.1993
   Add all the numbers of the birth date
   0+5+1+2+1+9+9+3 = 30 which is a 3 (as 3 + 0 = 3)
2. Steve's Birthday is 13. 08. 1972
   1+3+0+8+1+9+7+2 =31=(3+1) = 4

What's your Soul Path Number?

Soul Path 1: To learn independence, confidence and strength.

Soul Path 2: To learn about cooperating and supporting others.

Soul Path 3: To learn to express yourself and your creativity. Communication is key.

Soul Path 4: To learn practicality and self-discipline.

Soul Path 5: To learn adaptability and freedom.

Soul Path 6: To learn community and family responsibility.

Soul Path 7: To learn wisdom. Study and research is important in your life.

Soul Path 8: To learn about balance so you can gain success.

Soul Path 9: To learn about compassion so you can make the world brighter.

Divine Number:

Calculate your Divine Number by adding up the letters of your first name.

This reveals your focus in life.

Use your full name at birth (ie. What's on your birth certificate).

Or, if your name has changed, do two charts, one for each name and see what it reveals.

The Divine Number is where your birthname becomes a number. Use the grid below to help you.

1	2	3	4	5	6	7	8	9
A	B	C	D	E	F	G	H	I
J	K	L	M	N	O	P	Q	R
S	T	U	V	W	X	Y	Z	

Figure 11.1

Mother Teresa was born in Macedonia in 1910. Her birth name was *Agnes Gonxha Bojaxhiu.* She joined the Sisters in Ireland and later moved to India where she took vows to become a Nun. Mother Teresa received the Nobel Peace Prize in 1979.[18] Mother Teresa became Saint Mother Teresa in 2016.

A	G	N	E	S
1	7	5	5	1

=19

1 + 9 = 10 = 1

'Agnes' equals 1 which is an independent number. This number represents strength, leadership and persistence.

Divine Number:

1. Start with your first name only
2. Pick the first name which you were given at birth. My friend is called Paddy but his birth name is Patrick.

So his birth name destiny number is:

P	A	T	R	I	C	K
7	1	2	9	9	3	2

= 33 = (3+3) 6

Jessica is:

J	E	S	S	I	C	A
1	5	1	1	9	3	1

= 21 = 3

Divine Number 1: You will have an independent and determined focus in life.

Divine Number 2: You will have a cooperative and friendly focus in life.

Divine Number 3: You will have an expressive and creative focus in life.

Divine Number 4: You will have a practical and sensible focus in life.

---

18 biographyonline.net/nobelprize

Divine Number 5: You will have a flexible and resilient focus in life.

Divine Number 6: You will have a nurturing and caring focus in life.

Divine Number 7: You will have a mindful and expressive focus in life.

Divine Number 8: You will have a productive and courageous focus in life.

Divine Number 9: You will have a compassionate and empathetic focus in life.

Celestial Number:

Celestial Number is about the overall theme in your life.
This number is determined by adding your **Soul Path Number** and your **Divine Number** and reducing that total to a single digit.

Your Soul Path is what you're learning, your **Divine Number** is the way you deal with your lessons. The Celestial number is both numbers combined to reveal your overall response to life as you venture through it.

Celestial Number is calculated by Soul Path Number and Divine Number and reducing the total number to a single digit.

For example, Jessica's Soul path number was 3 and her Divine number was also three so her Celestial number will be 6.

Celestial Number 1: Independence and freedom will be your overall theme in life.

Celestial Number 2: Cooperation and motivation will be your overall theme in life.

Celestial Number 3: Self-expression and creativity will be your overall theme in life.

Celestial Number 4: Productivity and self-discipline will be your overall theme in life

Celestial Number 5: Freedom and Success will be your overall theme in life.

Celestial Number 6: Family and nurturing will be your overall theme in life.

Celestial Number 7: Mindfulness and philosophy will be your overall theme in life.

Celestial Number 8: Balance and integrity will be your overall theme in life.

Celestial Number 9: Charity and Goodwill will be your overall theme in life.

"It is not how much we do,
but how much love we put in the doing.
It is not how much we give,
but how much love we put in the giving."
Mother Teresa[19]

---

19 http://www.biographyonline.net/nobelprize/mother_teresa.html

CHAPTER 12

Shamanic Healing & Power Animals

"Challenges are initiations that facilitate our growth towards the light."[20]

A shaman is a natural spirit communicator. A person who looks to the sky and knows they are one with the stars, the planets and the air they breathe. A shaman is tuned in with nature and heals using natural remedies.

The universe uses the spirit of animals, birds, rocks and crystals to communicate to us. The Earth itself is a spirit that is loving towards us. We are made from the earth and we return to the earth to replenish the planet. Our spirit returns to the cosmos. Yet on some level it's all intertwined.

A shaman connects with spirit beings and beings in nature such as crystals, flowers, trees, mountains and sky. A shaman has a deep

---

20 Ingerman, S. (2014) *Walking in the Light* (p.100) Sounds True, Colorado.

love of nature and often connects with the earth, sky and spirits. A shaman likes to peacefully resolve conflict and likes to use heart-focused energy to harmonise with people and energy. A shaman is a natural healer who sees the mind, body and soul as being the most potent healer of all. The shaman ingests natural foods and liquids to maintain a healthy vibration and balance in life. A shaman easily smiles as their heart is open, full of gratitude and peace.

Shamanic Spirit

Everything is energy and everything has a vibration. When you communicate with a person you relate to them through thoughts and words. It's the same with other living energies such as crystals, plants, stones, animals, mountains, flowers, birds and trees. You can tap into their energy, and spirit, to help you.

You do not need to have the item or physical animal with you, on this physical plane, to connect to it's power. For example, you can call in the spirit energy of a bear to help give you strength. In my meditations I sometimes see a bear in my mind's eye, along with my other guides. I saw the bear around me for a few months to help give me strength and to help me focus on some of my projects. I enjoyed the presence of the bear and I thanked the bear for assisting me.

At other times, other animal totems would appear in my vision such as birds, snakes and fish. They turn up to assist me for a reason. I close my eyes and tune into their presence and energy. I ask them why they are around me. Sometimes they help me get more balance in my life or help me to heal my heart.

Shamanic Journeying

Shamanic journeying takes people on an inner world of discovery and allows us to see what is going on in our subconscious. After many years of doing healings with clients I realised that when I took clients on a visualisation it was as if I was also watching the vision unfold. I am shown and guided as to what visualisation to take the client on. After our journeying I'm in awe of the client's review of what visions they also had within the vision. It's like spirit allows both of our consciousness to merge, and in doing so we are gifted with a soul journey that reveals what we need to know.

My client George said to me, after one such journey, "That was amazing, you channelled that didn't you?" "Yes," I replied, "I am shown a vision and I relay this vision to you using my intuition, and spirits help, to see what's holding you back."

When the client is journeying they are also in a deeply, relaxed trance-like state, which allows them to go into their subconscious and super-conscious. We can release blocked energies from the past and move forward in more peaceful and harmonious ways. When the time is right you will be able to let go, forgive and move on. If you are unable to forgive that's alright. Take your time. Trauma and pain are challenging to face. It will all happen when your heart is ready. Shine love and light on the shadows of your past and step forward with new energy, new wisdom and new goals in your life.

"The shaman is the 'wounded healer', one who has experienced and survived many ordeals, or 'deaths', and returns to the community to share acquired healing wisdom to others."[21]

Exercise: Shaman Healing Journey

1. Light a candle and put oils/incense on if you wish. Relax and feel comfortable.

2. Breathe deeply into your heart several times.

3. Go to a magical garden full of flowers, cleansing waterfalls and beauty. You can smell the floral scents around you as you watch the

---

21 Wolf, L. (2009) *Shamanic Breathwork* (p.236) Bear & Company, Vermont.

beautiful waterfall cascade and flow down into the lagoon below. You look around and see your totem animal approach you.

4. You telepathically ask them any questions you need answered.

5. Go to an area where there is a path to the lower world. Deeper and deeper you go till you come to a crystal cave. You see a healing table and lie down. You are ready to heal and be nurtured. You deeply relax as your soul is restored.

6. You leave the crystal cave and return to the path where you see a golden vine going higher and higher into the sky. As you hold onto this vine, streams of rainbow colours gently elevate you up into the upper world. In the upper world you meet your higher self and your main guide.

7. You sit in a serene room and discuss with them what you need. They help you to gain clarity about what future steps to take. You feel loved and secure.

Shaman's 3 worlds

A Shaman has 3 worlds – the lower world, middle world and upper world. This is called the trinity of shamanism. The lower world includes animals and nature. Totem and Power animals belong in this lower world but they can also belong to the other worlds. The middle world is our current reality. The upper world is where shamans meet with spirit guides and higher beings. The three worlds are symbolised by a tree.

Each world contains its own vibration. The levels can to be accessed by a shaman when they are in an altered state of consciousness. These relaxed, or altered states, are called trance states. Trance states are achieved through meditation, yoga, drumming, rattles, dancing, chanting or deep breathing. The shaman is able to travel through these three worlds to ask, and receive, the information they need.

All three worlds are important and valuable, just like all parts of a tree make the whole. When we look at the roots of a tree we can understand the trunk. When we peer at the trunk of a tree we can understand the branches. Sometimes we need to step back to get a view of the whole tree to receive insights. We become like a flowing river of consciousness absorbing the gems in each of the three worlds.

Table 12.1

3 Worlds	Tree Symbology	Represents
Lower world	Roots	Lower world is a place of nature such as plants, minerals, animal, mountain and oceans. Power animals and plant totems are here. In the lower world there are divine spiritual essences of the natural world that we can commune with. The roots of the lower world absorb the nutrients which recharge the whole tree. Links to our unconscious and subconscious.

3 Worlds	Tree Symbology	Represents
Middle world	Trunk	The middle world is our current waking consciousness. This world tests and challenges us. This world gives us great wisdom and blessings too. If we are grounded in the lower world we can bring up nourishment to this level and the next. The middle world is said to be our ego, or conscious self.
Upper world	Branches	The upper world is called the celestial world. It's where the spirit guides, Angels and Higher Beings exist. The upper world is where we go for spiritual guidance and wisdom. The upper world is our true nature and divinity. It's where the branches of the tree flower to express the true beauty and brilliance of each soul. The upper world is our higher self and our super-consciousness which contains all time and space.

Exercise: 3 Worlds

1. Breathe deeply 10 times to take your brain rhythm into a relaxed state.

2. Imagine a crystal tower which is divided into 3 levels.

3. You walk into the lower level and take time to connect with nature and your inner self that is linked with your subconscious. You allow the lower world to commune with your heart. What do you see, hear, feel?

4. You take the stairs up to the middle world. You see what you are doing at present. You're shown what your ego and conscious self is thinking and doing right now. You allow the middle world to commune with your heart. What do you see, hear, feel and know?

5. You now ascend up more stairs until you reach the top of the crystal tower to where the upper world is. The upper world is our higher

self and our super-consciousness. You take time to rest and relax as you allow the upper world to commune with your heart. What do you see, hear, feel and know?

Shamanic Crystal Healing

Gloria had made amazing changes in her life since her last appointment. She viewed life differently now and decided it was time for another level of healing.

Gloria randomly chose 5 crystals from my crystal collection and then laid on the massage table as I covered her with blankets. Music played softly in the room. I placed the crystals on her body and used a pendulum to ascertain how her chakras were spinning.

The Heart chakra was struggling to spin as I noticed the pendulum was moving vertically. I laid my hands on Gloria and telepathically asked her heart: "Why are you struggling?"

I sensed grief in her heart. I silently asked the Reiki to help Gloria release the grief that was blocking her heart. I used my Shamanic rattles to help the chakras release stuck energy. I opened my third eye and called in more energy.

I saw a large bird hovering over Gloria's legs. To my surprise, I noticed the bird was actually a Pterosaur (flying reptile)! I asked the Pterosaur why was it there.

"I am here to help her tap into her ancient wisdom. We will do a lot of work together in the next 3–4 months."

After the Reiki, Gloria sat back down in her chair. I told her about my vision of the Pterosaur. We looked up this totem animal in a dream/symbol book which stated, "Dinosaur: Ancient part of self; can be used creatively or destructively." Gloria was being challenged by events in her life so we discussed how she perceived these experiences and how she could make better choices so that she could move forward more easily in her life.

Shamans see challenging events as initiations. When we pass that challenge, or initiation, we then progress to the next one. It's a bit like being at school or university. When we pass the exams, we can then move onto the next level.

What is your initiation teaching you? Why has your spirit called this experience into your life? What will you gain from it? Can you create an outcome that is win/win?

Exercise: Inner Child Sounds

Many of us have a wounded inner child that lives within us. Your inner child may become reactive if he/she feels left out, rejected or treated unfairly. At times your inner child behaves in reactive ways by fighting, being rebellious, self-sabotaging and acting like a victim. The best way to handle this part of ourselves is to lovingly parent the inner child within us.

Part 1 – Heal Yourself

1. Relax and breathe deeply a few times as you feel yourself becoming comfortable and peaceful. Feel connected to the sky above and the deep earth below you. Repeat several times.

2. Take your attention to your heart area in the centre of your chest.

3. Feel the amazing energy of your heart. Tune into your heart area and thank your heart for the ability to pump litres of blood around your body continuously.

4. Visualise your heart and how it has 3 chakras above and 3 chakras below it.

5. Ask your body which part of it needs healing. Wait for an answer. Make a sound while focusing your attention on this area. (If you are unsure of an area that's fine, just begin to hum so your whole

body resonates with this humming vibration. Trust that your body will intuitively know what sounds to release from your mouth and body.) Relax and enjoy this experience and allow the sounds to flow out of you. Your soul sound will help to heal the chakras and release any blockages or tension in them.

6. Now make an Aaaaa sound. This is the sound of the heart. Allow this sound to permeate your being. Become one with this sound.

Part 2 – Find your Inner Child

1. Go into your heart centre and imagine you are in a natural sanctuary and call in your inner child. Connect with your inner child in your heart area. Get a sense of how your inner child is feeling.

2. Imagine lovingly holding and tenderly hugging your inner child. Tell your inner child that you will keep them safe, that they are unique and special and that you will work with them so you can both achieve your dreams and goals. Ask your inner child if it is ready to forgive past hurts so that you can both release the past and be free to manifest your desires.

3. If the inner child needs time to heal that is fine. Repeat this exercise until you feel your inner child is at peace with the past or, see a healer or therapist that can help to give you extra support and loving guidance.

Part 3 – Hold Your Child

1. Imagine inside your heart an image of yourself and your inner child holding hands and being connected to one another. See both of you looking into each other's eyes and connecting to your dreams, passions and goals. Know that you will support each other and help to guide each other on the journey ahead.

2. Surround yourself in golden white light as you say to yourself. "I am connected on all levels of my Soul. I am protected and Divinely loved."

Power Animals and Energies

When I see power animals around people I tune in to find the reason and purpose the animal is present. For example, a dolphin may be in someone's aura as it's there to provide playfulness and flow in that person's life. A bird may be there to provide new ideas and help the person to fly!

Your power animal doesn't have to be a real animal as mythical animals often reveal themselves as totems too. Dolphins and mermaids work in harmony together. They cultivate harmony in our lives and instill the importance of looking after our environment. Dolphins encourage us to use our sixth sense as our intuition is our spiritual Guide in life. Unicorns have been mentioned in ancient texts and history books. It is believed unicorns had once roamed India and that they were like an ox or rhinoceros shape with an horn protruding from the head area.

Unicorns are known for their healing powers. The horn on a unicorn is said to hold healing and medicinal abilities to help those who call on its incredible powers. I find when I call the Spirit of a Unicorn in I feel teary as its third eye blends with my third eye. My brain waves seem to slow down as I feel its energy and wisdom going to areas in my body that need healing and rebalancing. Sometimes I hear sounds and messages as the unicorn's energy seems to open my ear chakras.

I remember reading once for a lady called Claire who had done a lot of healing courses and had researched extensively into shamanism. Claire came to me for a reading at an expo. I saw many animals and energies around her aura. Her consciousness had called them in. It was inspiring to see the shamanic energy surround and support her with so much love, insight and wisdom.

Bird Talk

My client Joanna said she understands bird talk. She went outside her house once when a magpie squawked at her.

She said she knew the bird was telling her that her son had been injured. Not long after her son arrived home with an injury from a bike accident.

Joanna had been able to interpret the message the bird was giving to her.

Totem Animals

Here is a list of totem animals and their meanings. This is just a guide, use your own intuition to search for the right meaning that resonates for you. Channel the energy of the animal and receive the wisdom and gifts they have to offer. You may like to write up your own list of animals and their meanings.

ALLIGATOR: assertiveness, charging ahead

ANT: group effort, take action

BAT: secretly making your mark, be still and focus, surrender

BEAR: protector, healing, strength, wisdom, change; hibernate and tune into higher energies

BEAVER: builder, creator, power

BIRDS: messenger, trust, freedom

BUFFALO: sacredness, life, abundance and gratitude

BUTTERFLY: metamorphosis, transformation and expansion

CAT: independent, mystical, loving, cautious

COYOTE: clever, skilled

CROW: shape shifting, adaptability

DEER: gentle, caring, kind

DOG: noble, loyal, leader

DOLPHIN: introspective, stillness, flow, balance, harmony

DRAGON: our past, subconscious, deep understanding

DRAGONFLY: transcend, rebirth

EAGLE: spiritual energy, connection to energies, patience

FOX: cunning, liveliness, well-planned

FROG: flexible, vitality

HAWK: messenger, intuition

HORSE: endurance, faithfulness, moving ahead

LION: powerful, a seeker

LIZARD: resilience, smart

MOOSE: clear headed, determined

MOUSE: order, organiser

OTTER: playful, prophetic

OWL: clairvoyance, insight, clarity, moon energy

PORCUPINE: virtue, companionship, hope

RABBIT: hope, humble, creative

RAVEN: courage, knowledge

SEAHORSE: confidence, beauty, presence

SHARK: hunter, flexibility, decisive

SKUNK: reputation, presence, strength

SNAKE: rebirth, kundalini, magic

SPIDER: manifest own web in life, making decisions

SQUIRREL: designer, collector

SWAN: grace, balance and centredness

TURTLE: nurturer, caring, safe

UNICORN: visions, universal energies

WHALE: perceptive, motivated

WOMBAT: dig deep within and find the strength to power on & create healthy boundaries

WOLF: faithful, persistent, successful, good communicator

CHAPTER 13

Past Lives, Akashic Records & Spirit Releasement

The **Akashic records** are a library of thoughts, events, and emotions of our past, present and future.

To access the records I picture a gigantic library that houses all wisdom and knowledge. Some people chant a certain verse or phrase to access the records while others do meditations.

When I visualise the Akashic records I find there is a librarian ready to help assist me find information from the records. Not all records are available for public viewing though as a person's soul may need to discover the answers for themselves.

Exercise: Accessing Akashic Records

1. Relax and breathe deeply as this will allow you to drop into an alpha /theta state so you can access the records.

2. Surround yourself with a bright white light that is protective, loving and peaceful. You are safe and surrounded by love.

3. Imagine you are walking into an amazing library. There are many shelves of beautifully bound books. Each book has writing on its spine. You walk in and wait at the desk. The librarians walk around and whisper. One will approach you when ready. They take you to a desk and ask you what you want to know from the records. You answer them from your heart.

4. They write your answer on a slip of paper and it disappears into thin air. Before you know it you are walking down an aisle with an Advanced librarian. This means that your request has been granted and they will assist you to find your information. You follow the Advanced librarian to a row of books. One of the books flashes a gold colour and they open this book up. You see words, images and movies as the book reveals its records to you. You absorb the information and nod when you are finished. The Advanced librarian smiles at you, bows and you are automatically outside the library.

5. What did you learn? Write it down if you wish.

Remember that a part of us wants certain answers from the records so, remember to be clear minded and respect whatever the records show. Your own wishes, hopes and dreams can influence how you interpret the records. Allow the information to come to you. If no information appears or you are not allowed to see the records, understand that they honour your free will and do not want to interfere with your progress, growth and development at this point in time.

Past Lives

Most of us do not remember our past lives, however it is possible to access some information through a guided past life session.

People have different experiences in a past life session. A friend of mine found themself speaking in a foreign language! Others may have flashbacks or wonder how they knew about something. One night I awoke in the middle of a dream and I could see a mini movie screen playing in front of my eyes. The bedroom was dark yet I could see this movie screen about 30cm in front of my face. It showed an army plane flying over rocky mountains. I was a nurse on the plane. I feel it was a past life memory.

That was interesting as I always wanted to be a nurse. I ended up being a naturopath so it was close!

My friend Danielle saw a past life image of where she had drowned, in the ocean, in a previous lifetime. It helped Danielle to understand why she had to get over her deep fear of swimming in this lifetime.

A client may ask for a past life session in the hope of finding out more about themselves in this lifetime. Sometimes I am shown a client's past life appearing around their aura. This little image usually appears on the right side of their head, about 10–20cm out from their head area. When I focus on the past life image I get shown more information which I then share with a client. Some clients say they have dreamt about what happened to them in another lifetime. Other clients reveal they feel particularly drawn to certain time periods and feel they may have once lived in that time.

Exercise: Anna's Past Lives Meditation

You will need:

A chair or comfortable place to sit or lie down

A blanket or cover as some people's body temperature drops

Loose clothing

Preparation:

1. Make yourself feel comfortable and relaxed. Loosen any clothing.

2. Stay in your heart. Feel relaxed. Remember the more you practise the deeper you go.

3. You are safe and in control. This is a time for you to get insight, messages and understanding. Tap into your subconscious and superconscious. Whatever comes to you is fine.

4. Remember, at any time, you can float above and watch any images or scenes, just like you are watching a movie.

Exercise: Past Lives Meditation

1. Breathe in joy and peace and breathe out love and peace.

2. Breathe in a healing golden white light energy to make you feel safe and deeply relaxed. Allow this golden white light to permeate you in a loving and connected way. This guiding light feels warm, connected and ancient.

3. As you breathe in and out, focus on your jaw and feel it deeply relax, letting go and feeling free and light. Now relax the muscles in your face.

4. Relax the neck and shoulders feeling calm and peaceful.

5. Allow the waves of golden white light energy to penetrate each and every cell, surrounding them with deep relaxation, peace and tranquillity. Relax your chest and heart, knowing that any background noises will allow you to go deeper and deeper. Relax your arms, your fingers, your palms. Relax your upper back as you go deeper into a level of serenity and peace.

6. The golden white healing light continues to relax your lower back muscles, your internal organs and it lovingly continues down your legs, relaxing and rejuvenating your whole body to perfect health and wellness. This amazingly gentle, yet powerful light,

flows down to your feet and soles helping you to go deeper and deeper. Let's now go down 10 to 1 so you go deeper, so deep that you can remember experiences that will teach you and help you. Go 10, 9, 8 go deeper 7, 6, 5 deeper 4, 3 peace and serenity, 2, 1 to a divine state of calm.

7. Go to a gorgeous garden where there are flowers, beauty and peace. This beautiful sanctuary is a safe place where you can heal, release and step into your true self.

8. Silently count down from 5 to 1. Go back to your early childhood. You can remember everything. Allow information to come to you easily. Stay in your heart and perceive accurately what you need to remember. 5, find a pleasurable memory, as you get to the number 4, you can remember it all clearly, remember your childhood. As you count down to 3, 2, 1 you see the details and location.

9. What are you aware of, what do you look like ?

10. What do you hear, see, taste, smell? Go deeper to focus the detail clearly. Take a few more breaths so it will become sharper and more focused.

11. Whatever comes to you is fine so pay attention to the details so you can remember more, float above if need be, feel free. Allow yourself to understand why you chose that memory – it is trying to tell you something. Why is it important to you now? (Take note of the memory or, if guiding someone else through this past life meditation have the person share what they see, hear, feel etc).

12. Now go back to the beautiful garden. You're ready to go back to before your birth, when you are in your mother's womb.

13. Going down from 5 to 1.
    5, 4, 3, 2, 1. You are now in your mother's womb, feel your emotions and sense your parents' energies.

14. Why did you choose your parents? Why are you returning back to the Earth plane?

15. Thank yourself for your insights.

16. You are now ready to go further back to your past lives. You are safe and secure. At any time you can float above any memories or images that come to you.

17. Relax and go deeper and deeper. Now imagine and visualise a door to your past lives. Again counting 5, 4, 3, 2, 1, you will see the door open. You walk through it and you see a bright welcoming light and on the other side of the light you see a person or a scene from a past life and you'll remember everything.

18. What are they doing? Sense the energy, is it familiar to you? Do you know or recognise the people around you? What is your sex, age, occupation? What happened during your life? What was your life lesson?

19. Go forward in this life. What did you learn from that lifetime?

20. Now you are ready to experience another lifetime. 1, 2, 3 you are there in another time, another lifetime. Another experience. What are you aware of? Are there other people around you? Do you recognise them, are they familiar to you in anyway?

21. Explore other details, events and memories in that life to help you heal. Be aware of shapes, colours and styles. Notice the history, the culture, geography. Notice the buildings around you, how others are dressed. What are they doing? Sense the energy, is it familiar to you? Do you know or recognise the people around you? What is your sex, age, occupation? What happened during your life? What was your life lesson? Go forward in this life. What did you learn from that lifetime? Imagine yourself floating into a beautiful space, so peaceful.

22. Now you are ready to go to a magical garden. Imagine a beautiful spiritual being such as your Higher Self, Guide, Angel, a wise or loving being who comes to visit you in this garden. You can communicate mind to mind to see if they have any messages for you, any knowledge or wisdom to help you remove blocks from your current life and to feel more joyful.

23. What can they tell you or show you? Take time to enjoy their energy and presence. You will remember the messages they give to you.

24. Return to full waking consciousness, you will remember everything: the child, the womb, the birth, the other lifetimes and the message.

25. Remember you are always loved and you are never alone, you are filled with a splendid, peaceful energy. Be grounded in your body and back in your full waking consciousness. Be awake and alert.

26. Counting 1 to 10 – feeling more awake, feeling great when you get to 10.

1, 2, 3 feeling calm and at peace

4, 5, 6 more awake, feeling great, feeling wonderful

7, 8, 9, 10. Good, eyes open, stretch. Come back to full alertness.

Note: Past Life Regression is good to do with a practitioner familiar with Past Life Regression techniques.

Spirit Releasement and House Clearing

The spirits who attach, or hover near our auras, can help or hinder us. These spirits may be around our energy field, or homes, if the vibration is similar to theirs. Usually the more positive your energy the more positive the spirits are around you.

Spirit beings can teach us to look at our thought patterns, beliefs and behaviours. There are many wonderful spirit energies that walk beside us and help us in life.

However, there are other spirits that attach for other reasons. Some spirits hang around our auras due to emotions such as fear or behaviours such as addictions. When we heal and change the negative spirit normally leaves, as the vibration of the person's energy no longer resonates with the lower vibrations.

An Unwelcome Guest

I remember when Lily came to see me. She said there was a dark energy in her home. I saw an image of a negative energy in the second end room of her house.

I communicated with this dark spirit and he was very chatty. I asked him why he was in Lily's home. He said Lily's negative thinking and obsessive thoughts were making him feel quite comfortable and at home in the room.

Lily and I discussed her emotions and she learnt to face her fears about her relationship. Over time the energy in her home returned to its peaceful state.

By using **Spirit Releasement** we can assist any spirit to transition or cross over into a different realm. Since all attached spirits have a similar emotion as those experienced by their human hosts – we need only figure out the emotional issue and then we can effectively move the spirit on.

Just asking the client what's going on in their lives will bring up the deep feelings and buried emotions that will help us tap into the energy we need to look at and heal. Once a client talks about these issues the vibration and energy field will shift so the spirit attachment may simply choose to leave.

In Spirit Releasement sessions, my aim is to help both the client and the spirit. I do not send negative words or behaviour to the spirit as it also needs love and guidance. Like attracts like. A firefly will go to the street lamp because that is what it is naturally drawn to. It's the same with any other energies.

You can help an attached Spirit to move on but, if a client continues drinking alcohol, taking drugs, entertaining a negative mindset or other behaviour that lowers their energy, then the spirit may return to happily attach to that vibration again.

Those who need a Spirit Releasement session usually feel out of sorts. Many feel there is a Spirit, or heavy energy, attached to their aura. We are all made of energy so earthbound Spirits, who are lost and unhealed in their own turmoil, may attach to someone with a similar vibration. Once you have a spirit attachment you may find it difficult to make choices and it feels like something else is controlling you and making you stay in bad habits and addictions.

So how do we release these encounters?

In order to help you perform the Spirit Releasement call upon your own guides and angels for protection and assistance. You may also like to see someone experienced in spirit releasement to help you. Usually I find if a person wants to clean up their thoughts, and their life, then their vibration will change and these Spirits are unable to attach as the aura is stronger and more resilient. All attached Spirits are there for a reason. They also deserve love as most of them do not believe they are lovable or worthy of love. When we release the Spirits we want to send them to a place of love and healing.

Dan's Spirits

Dan regularly consumed drugs and alcohol. His energy was low and he was badly treated by a family member when he was a child. The scars from his childhood ran deep.

Dan was living in ways that weakened his aura and energy. This made him more susceptible to wandering spirits. It's no surprise that alcohol is also called a "spirit!"

I looked at Dan's aura and saw a shadow near the left-hand side of his body. I told Dan I sensed a spirit attachment. Before I could say where, Dan said " I know, it's over here isn't it?" as he pointed to the left side of his body.

"Yes" I replied. Dan was intuitive enough to already sense where the energy was.

Through our sessions together, Dan took time to unpack the heavy baggage of his childhood. Over time his aura and energy changed. He changed his thoughts, which led to a change in his actions and behaviours.

"Anna I've decided to forgive what happened to me in my past," he told me at the end of a session one day. "I'm sick and tired of living under a rock. I want to wake up and feel good about life."

After he made the decision to let go of his anger and resentment his soul lightened up and he no longer required his addictions.

By inviting in new habits and thoughts he was also allowing in more of his Soul essence and more joy and vitality. Dan did not need alcohol or drugs to numb his feelings any more. He realised his shift in life brought a new awakening, a new peace and the power to have more fun than he ever imagined.

Dan later met a lovely partner and embarked on a new life with more clarity, self-esteem and integrity.

It's believed that people who died, like an alcoholic for example, may hang around this Earth plane and continue their drinking by attaching to someone who drinks a lot. Alcohol is a poison and puts great strain on the organs and energy of the body.

Remember a spirit is just an energy like us.

We all have periods in our life where we feel ill or unwell. This does not mean a Spirit will latch onto you. There's sometimes no rhyme or reason. However, if you find that you are feeling a spiritual presence draining your energy start by asking them to move on. Often simply acknowledging them may be enough to change the energy.

Request, three times, for the spirit to kindly go to a portal of light and send so much love and kindness to this spirit in the hope that they heal on their journey as well, as we are all here to learn, grow, love and evolve.

Healing Heavy Energy

Thought forms can attach too. I remember coming home from work one day and, for some reason, my mind kept thinking about a co-worker, Leah. I had noticed in the staff room that Leah had been rude and cold to others at work. For some reason an image of Leah would pop up in my mind when I was at home.

I decided to do something about it, as I was beginning to feel annoyed. I stopped, closed my eyes and imagined Leah's energy. I saw in my mind's eye a picture of Leah and I asked her telepathically, "What's going on?"

Her energy and vibration responded to me energetically and I sensed her saying: "I'm really frustrated and annoyed. Life is confusing. I keep going around in circles."

"Why are you in my mind?" I queried.

"I want to be more free. I feel so weighed down. I want to work part-time."

I opened my heart and sent her love, peace and joy. I knew that Leah has free will about whether to accept my good will or not. Intuitively I felt Leah embraced the offering. I instantly felt lighter. Even the image of Leah in my mind seemed happier and more content. I felt her spirit sigh a sense of relief. My thoughts about this co-worker soon subsided and I felt more warmth and connection to her.

I returned to work the next week and I heard that Leah had changed her work to part-time hours. She no longer worked full-time and seemed happier for it.

Hallway Spirit

Natasha was a pretty brunette with warm blue eyes. During the session Natasha shared that she couldn't sleep well at night because she felt there was an energy in her home. I asked my guides, in my mind, to show me information about her house.

I saw a dark area in the middle of the house. I ascertained that this was a hallway. I said to Natasha that I felt the spirit was in her hallway. She opened her eyes wide, "Yes it is!"

Natasha explained that the spirit did not go into her room but she would hear footsteps going up and down the hallway at nighttime. Natasha was going to bed very late as she was too scared to go to sleep earlier as the noise frightened her.

I tuned into the energy of the house and picked up an elderly man. We did a mental clearing and healing for her home and I also gave her some sage to take home and cleanse her house.

Natasha later told me that she now sleeps better as the hallway noises had ceased.

Exercise to Release Spirits

1. A simple method is to imagine a portal on the ceiling above you. The portal may look like a round or triangular opening which is filled with the most Divine Golden Rays of Heavenly light.

2. Tell the spirit to go to the light and inform the energy that is it loved and that when they go towards the portal of light they will be cared for and protected.

3. Repeat this request three times.

This is a simple but powerful technique.

Exercise: House and Space Clearing Ideas

Houses, and buildings, can hold negative or positive energy in them. You may notice a room feels different after an argument or dispute. There are ways to clear and cleanse this energy by using one or more of the ideas below.

- Imagine a Crystal in the room or around yourself. Your thoughts are real and powerful so imagining crystals is an amazing way to clear a room.

- Visualise colours in the space and around yourself. The colour that you intuitively visualise will protect you and help your aura to recharge and revitalise.

- Burn incense or aromatherapy oils to shift and cleanse areas in a home.

- Spray essences around the room. You can make up your own essential oil essences. I have bottles of essences around my home which I use as a mist which are very refreshing. I make these spray essences by using cooled boiled water and then I intuitively add a few drops of my favourite essential oils.

- Also you can make crystal elixirs to help the vibration of the area too (see details in Chapter 15).

- Play uplifting music as each chakra has a musical vibration. Music will help to harmonise the body (endocrine glands) and therefore your whole being will feel more relaxed.

- Use chimes, crystal bowls or bells to activate new energy in the room and make it feel crisp, clear and divine!
- Meditate in the room to fill your aura with more energy which will expand into the space around you.
- Put Reiki energy and symbols in the room as these will attract a new state of energy to the surrounding environment.
- Design a crystal grid in the room. Find a flat surface where you can make a pattern with your crystals. Some people add flower petals, pictures or pebbles to their grid. Be creative and feel the amazing energy that crystal grids can activate and produce.

Blue Fire Activation:

While reading this book, you will be activated in Blue Fire Healing energy. It will only activate if it's right for your heart and Soul. I had not planned this but, while writing this chapter, I felt a strong urge to let you know about Blue Fire so I let the information flow and wrote down its messages for you.

While it's activating you may feel tingles, a buzz or an energy flow around you or on your body. I am guided to share this loving, healing, energy with you. It's freely available if your consciousness believes it and trusts it. If you doubt it or feel it's not real then it will respect your wishes and be activated and used elsewhere. Your free will is of paramount importance to the Higher Energies and Beings.

As you rest or sleep at night ask this Blue Fire energy to heal you, your family, friends and our expansive universe. You deserve to be able to tap into this infinite healing energy. It is available and it comes with Miracles and powerful outcomes. Let go, believe and allow this to be a part of your life, your existence and your presence.

I asked for a symbol to be linked to Blue Fire. As I closed my eyes, and allowed information to come to me, I saw what looked like a

TV antenna in my 3rd eye. I then saw a divine blue-coloured Being behind it.

My arms began to tingle and my head moved slightly as the energy connected with me. "I am here to serve, dear Anna. Thank You for sharing this simple method." The Being said. "We are love Dear ones and as you share our Wisdom it will allow others to tap into the infinite energies of the cosmos. We are always with you all. It's an illusion that we leave you. We are always supporting you and praying for you. Have faith, hope and Love. We are a part of your life. Call us in, talk to us and commune with our Power. Our power is your power. We Go in peace to serve you and this world. And so it is, dear one."

Part 2

Healing
Techniques

CHAPTER 14

Hands-on Healing & Reiki

**The word *Reiki* is made of two Japanese words.
Rei which *means* the Higher Power and wisdom,
Ki means life force energy.**

Hands-on healing is available to everyone. My wish is for you to know that you can activate hands-on healing at any time. All you need is your intentions and to ask. By asking you allow the energies to flow through you. Your thoughts and your consciousness are powerful. What you think you create! I have been teaching Reiki for many years. It's a beautiful, graceful healing modality. It takes trust, openness and a belief in the power of the unseen world. When I first learnt Reiki I doubted its effectiveness "how could something so simple work so well." It took me a while to trust it, let go and believe in the power of the unseen world.

Reiki (pronounced RAY KEY) is a form of healing using divine energy channelled through the hands towards the aura of another to replenish their vitality. It is a non-evasive and comforting modality which is appropriate for all kinds of people with a variety of health issues.

Reiki began with a Japanese man called Mikao Usui (1865–1926). Usui was a highly spiritual man and one day he decided to meditate and fast, on a mountain in a rural area in Japan. During his fast he started to gain insights and enlightenment about the power of energy. After fasting one day he felt a strong powerful energy around him and from then Reiki was born.

Chujiro Hayashi was a student of Usui who began a Reiki clinic which was open until 1940. Dr Hayashi developed more Reiki techniques, and further knowledge, that he passed onto his students. Dr Hayashi was also responsible for the formal aspects of Reiki which are taught today – namely the hand positions and the science-based practises held within Reiki.

Hawayo Takata (1900–1980) lived in Hawaii but was of Japanese descent. Takata travelled to Japan to look for a doctor to help her heal and to get an operation. She went to Dr Hayashi's clinic and after several sessions of Reiki, Takata realised that she no longer needed surgery. She wanted to know how to do the healing treatment so Dr Hayashi taught her Reiki. A year later Takata returned to Hawaii to do her own healings. In the 1970s Takata taught students to become Reiki masters. These students continued to spread Reiki throughout the world.

"Energy is called kundalini, prana, or chi, depending on the culture or tradition encountered."[22]

In *Japanese*, energy is called Ki, in *Chinese* its Chi, in *Indian* it's Prana, to the *Native Americans* it's called the Great Spirit.
I have also loved teaching Reiki classes to children. When we teach others this simple modality we allow them to have faith and know that healing is only a palm away! The guides and Ki energy are always around.

---

22 Usui, M. & Petter, F. (2011) *The Original Handbook of Dr. Mikao Usui*, Lotus Press, USA.

Reiki energy is channelled down through our crown chakra. We do not use our own energy as we use Divine source which is always with us and is part of our cellular and energetic energy. Reiki is the laying of hands so we can all do it naturally. I feel it's a gift that we can all tap into. Hands-on healing uses your own palm chakras to bring through this divine energy. I advise clients to rest in bed at night and place their healing hands on their body. Try it now, place one of your hands on your body where you feel pain or tiredness and request the following:

"Divine Energy Please give me strength, relaxation and a restful sleep ahead."

Ask three times and then note how you feel.

Everything is connected so the Ki energy will go to wherever it needs to. The universal energy is supremely loving and is always around us.

Doing healing courses helps us to tap into the energy, practise and understand how it's done but, remember that hands-on healing is freely available to anyone at any time, so even if you have not done a course you can still tap into this potent healing.

Reiki Principles

The Reiki principles by Mikao Usui are:

Just for today, live the attitude of gratitude.

Just for today, do not worry.

Just for today, do not anger.

Just for today, do my work honestly.

Just for today, show love and respect to every living thing.

We may not always live up to these principles but they highlight the importance of living in the now with integrity, gratitude, honesty and respect.

How does Reiki Feel?

As energy flows through the body and aura, people may experience different sensations. Some people will feel warmth, heat, tingling or other sensations. Others just feel relaxed and may fall asleep.

Reiki is a healing experience that is unique for each person. The healing energy has an intelligence of its own. It knows where to go. All it needs is an open heart and a willingness to let go, just be and trust. The body is designed to heal itself.

You may notice that when you feel low in energy, or Chi, you feel flat and lethargic. When your chi is higher you feel happier and more vital. You can activate and increase your chi and energy through Reiki by putting your hands on yourself or, just imagining the healing life force energy flowing through you, increasing the chi in your body. You may even sense a colour or vibration while you do this.

Like meditation, Reiki and healing energy is cumulative, so it builds up each time you have a treatment. Maintaining good health, and Chi, by doing gentle exercises, eating and sleeping well will allow the energy to flow through well. The energy comes through a person from a higher source that the whole universe is made of. When you do a healing on another person you will receive a healing at the same time. This is a double blessing as the client, as well as yourself, will both be energised with chi energy.

The universal life force energy is available to everyone. It's a gift from the cosmos. Reiki is loving, energising and revitalising.

Reiki and laying of hands is one of the most loving things you can do for yourself. I use it more often now than when I originally learnt Reiki. My relationship with, and understanding of Reiki has grown so that my bond and connection with it is more trusting, real and alive. When you tap into the healing stream of Reiki you tap into an expansive universe that is wise, powerful and extremely loving. You deserve that energy. It belongs to you and by honouring it, and calling it in, it will become a magical part of your life and existence.

Your Reiki Treatment

In a Reiki healing session, the person sits or lays down fully clothed, eyes are usually closed. I like to have gentle soothing music on but you can ask the person if they would like silence or music on. I prefer music without words as I find this more soothing for the soul.

I remember many years ago going to a healer who had upbeat music on. The words and music were distracting. I did not ask her to turn it off as I decided to breathe deeply and go into my own space.

In hindsight I could have asked for the music to be turned off or had different music put on. I tell clients the space is theirs and I want them to feel comfortable.

I like to cover people with a light cover as I like to loosely tuck them in and make them feel snug. Allow people to wiggle at any time to adjust their body if need be. Also if the person in lying on their back I ask if they need an eye mask.

About half of my clients use an eye mask. I firstly fold a tissue in half and put it over their eyes then place a small eye pillow over their eyes. A small towel can be used as well. I also inform clients they can remove this cover at any time.

In hands-on healing, or Reiki, hands will be placed on the body. The hands will not touch private or personal areas such as genitals or breasts. Some people do not like their feet touched so check with them first. I have only ever had one client who requested that hands were placed above their body. In this case I did not touch the body but hovered my hands a few centimetres above them. This is fine and still very effective.

In most people your non-dominant hand is the hand that receives, or brings in energy. Your dominant hand (that you write with) gives out energy.

While receiving healing energy some people report feelings of heat, cold, tingling or shivers throughout their body. Some say they had no sensations but saw colours or images. Each experience is unique and perfect. Sometimes when I am giving Reiki the same happens to me. I may or may not get sensations, images or colours, guides, etc. I allow whatever needs to come through.

If I open my third eye I can see what's happening energetically around the person's body and in the room we are in. If a totem animal appears I will tell the clients afterwards and we will discuss why the energy of that animal is in their aura at this time. Reiki sends people into a state of deep relaxation as it relaxes our nervous system.

After a Reiki healing session some people may experience a loose stool the next day. This is a sign your body is letting go and is releasing. I encourage people to drink water, and herbal teas, to help cleanse their system.

Be aware of any thoughts or emotions you may have the days following a session. Be gentle with yourself and honour those thoughts and question why certain thought patterns or behaviours are coming up for you. Journal your thoughts and feelings so that you can further discover more about yourself and the way you tick.

Reiki on Rosa

I had an elderly client, Rosa who had been a smoker for many years. Although she was told by Doctors to stop smoking years ago, she did not give them up until a lung cancer diagnosis came her way. Although Rosa found it a challenge to get up and down from the massage table, she loved Reiki and the visualisations we did.

I offered to give Rosa Reiki in the chair but she loved lying on the table so I was happy to assist her getting up and down the massage table. I informed Rosa that hands-on healing can be done by anyone. Rosa was keen to learn this simple technique so I showed her how to lay hands on herself.

Rosa enjoyed using the healing energy at home on herself. She said it eased her pain and helped her to sleep better.

Exercise: Hands-on Healing Activation

1. Call in and activate the healing energy and ask that it assists you on any level whether it's emotional, spiritual, physical or mental. Know that the healing outcome will be for your Highest good.

2. Close your eyes if you wish, and place your palms on your body.

3. Feel and sense what's happening.

4. Breathe deeply and slowly and allow the healing to occur.

5. Take note of what happens.

6. Keep up the practise. Tap into the energy and bond with it. Hands-on healing is a tool that is free, simple, effective and is always with you!

I am a Reiki Master and have taught Reiki for many years. I have taught other people to also be Reiki teachers. I have designed a certified course called Psychic Reiki which combines Reiki levels with psychic intuitive knowledge.

Benefits of Reiki are:

- Reiki can benefit many levels of our being. Our physical, mental, emotional and spiritual parts of us.

- Reiki supports our innate healing process. Reiki brings peace, calmness and clarity. In Reiki we do not diagnose health issues unless we have professional qualifications.

- When using Reiki on yourself, and others, it helps reduce worry, fear and anxiety. Research has shown that Reiki, and hands-on healing, enables clients to feel a sense of wellbeing and safety as well as reducing pain and increasing their awareness.[23]

- When you use Reiki on another, there is a double blessing. It allows the life force energy to help heal the client and it is also activated in your energy field so it will stimulate a healing response in yourself too!

- Reiki can assist in many areas such as depression, insomnia, lack of confidence and addictions.

Many clients say Reiki, and hands-on healing, helps them to sleep better. Some people have more vivid dreams. After receiving Reiki some people's awareness and understanding about their issue, becomes clearer to them.

---

23 Usui, M. & Petter, F. (2011) *The Original Handbook of Dr. Mikao Usui*, Lotus Press, USA.

Research reveals that Reiki, and hands-on healing, is effective with helping anxiety, pain and depression. Studies have shown that Reiki helps the adrenals, spleen and nervous system. Reiki also helps reduce pain and helps people have more mobility in their body. [24]

Reiki and hands-on healing can:

- Release energy blocks
- Balance chakras (mind, body and spirit)
- Increase energy levels
- Produce deep relaxation and help the body release stress and tension
- Improve focus and clarity
- Lower blood pressure
- Reduce pain
- Cleanse body and detox the aura
- Help the immune system
- Awaken spiritual growth and emotional development
- Encourage creativity, new ideas and passions

Some clients tell me their doctor is happy they are receiving Reiki while other health practitioners are more sceptical. One client said her doctor encouraged the use of Reiki. This client benefitted from both conventional treatment and complementary medicine. Some clients throw away the pills from their doctor and use food and healing energy as their medicine. Remember, **do not** stop any medications unless you have seen your doctor or health care professional.

Healing Intentions

Your intention is important in healing. The reason why you do anything in life is paramount. For example, we can do chores with a

---

24 Usui, M. & Petter, F. (2011) *The Original Handbook of Dr. Mikao Usui*, Lotus Press, USA.

negative intention and mindset or, do chores with the intention of doing them to make life more enjoyable, pleasant and peaceful. A friend I know puts on music when she does the housework so that she can enjoy it. Also the music puts her in a better mind frame. Your mind frame when giving Reiki is important too. When giving Reiki energy intends that it is used for the Highest purpose of all concerned. If the person's Soul does not want Reiki then intend that the energy goes to wherever it is needed. Send energy for the highest good and trust that the Divine Intelligence of the cosmos knows where the energy goes and how it heals.

When I first began doing Reiki I wanted instant results. I wanted the client to feel better straight away. I was happy when the client leapt off the massage table and said "wow, my back pain is gone." Other times clients said they did not receive the instant healing they expected. I have since learnt that Reiki, and hands-on healing, has its own Divine intelligence. The healing can happen on different levels and in its own time frame. Sometimes people will heal in a day, a week, a month or a year as healing occurs on so many different levels. Giving healing from the heart, then letting go, is the most beautiful gift you can give to yourself and the recipient. Just your presence and being there for the receiver is healing and graceful in itself. Just love. Just be. To honour yourself, the person and the Ki is profoundly magical. My Master Reiki teaching manual says "Reiki is Intention." Know and believe that the energy is working and that your intentions are powerful in the process.

Remember what you believe in manifests. When you do hands-on healing give from your heart, allow the Higher energies to flow through you then let go. By letting go we trust that the Ki energy will do its healing in its own time and perfect pace for all concerned. Healing occurs on all levels spiritual, emotional, mental and physical. Although results may not be obvious immediately, know in your heart that Reiki energy continues to work long after the actual treatment is finished.

Grace's Reiki Healing

54-year-old Grace lay down on my Reiki table. I covered her with a light blanket and proceeded to lay my hands on her as the Reiki energy flowed. I opened my third eye to see the colours and images around her.

I saw a grey colour around her heart chakra, in the chest area of Grace's body. I tuned into the colour and sensed that age 12 was connected to this area of her body.

"What happened around the age of 12?" I asked her. Immediately Grace began to cry.

She explained that when she was 12 her family had moved to Australia from Holland. It had been a stressful and scary time for her. When her family arrived in Australia things did not go as smoothly as her parents had hoped.

Grace's heart was still holding onto the anxiety and fear that occurred at that age and these emotions were affecting her current relationships. I helped Grace to connect the dots between her adult life and the wounds of her childhood.

Grace resolved the emotions of her childhood and made peace with them. This healing helped the way she related to herself and others.

Reiki Techniques

I was delighted to read a book based on interviews with Usui, about different hand positions in Reiki.[25] In the interviews Usui discussed how he used massage, pressure and gentle tapping in his Reiki treatments. Usui also used his fingertips or the whole of his hand when healing. I also find using different techniques useful when giving Reiki healing.

---

25 Usui, M. & Petter, F. (2011) *The Original Handbook of Dr. Mikao Usui*, Lotus Press, USA.

With animals, hands-on healing can be done on or off their body depending on the mood & the temperament of the animal. My neighbour has two cats. One cat loves hands above the body while the other cat prefers to have hands on the body as she loves touch and smooches!

Note: In most people your non-dominant hand is the hand that receives or, brings in energy. Your dominant hand (that you write with) gives out energy.

Spine Tip

To help a client's energy, rub gently on either side of the spine. Start at the lower back and move up to the upper back. You may also like to press your fingertips along the spine area as well. Or you may like to use the base of your hands as this nice firm pressure is relaxing. Follow your intuition.

"Your hands know what is happening so learn to trust them."[26]

Breath Cycle

Breathe deeply and slowly as you do hands-on healing. Breathe in energy from the earth and the sky. Breathe in, simultaneously, earth energy up your legs (through your feet) while you also breathe in cosmic sky energy, into your crown chakra. Both these energies will fill your body and go out through your hands for healing. As you breathe in and out this wonderful cycle continues to expand your energy and aura.

This breathing cycle cleanses, heals and allows the energy to flow naturally and energetically. That is why, when you heal, you also receive the Divine source of energy as it ripples divinely through your body.

---

26 Usui, M. & Petter, F. (2011) *The Original Handbook of Dr. Mikao Usui,* (p.17) Lotus Press, USA.

Exercise: Healing Breath

1. Place your hands on (or above) self or another person, plant or pet. [Imagine doing this if you are doing distance healing].

2. Ask for healing. Knowing the healing energy will provide the perfect healing.

3. Intend for the healing energy to flow from your crown, down your arms and out through your palms.

4. Breathe in and imagine energy coming up through the soles of your feet while energy is coming in through the top of your head.

5. These energies fill your body with Divine light. As you breathe out the energy goes to where it needs to go.

6. Open up your senses, what colours, images, sounds do you receive?

Repeat the **Healing Breath** as you allow the rhythm of the breath to flow through your being. You are a vessel for healing. I thank you for activating this healing presence in your life to help yourself, others and the world.

Reiki Helps Transition

An old friend of mine, Dave, told me he used hands-on healing when his grandmother was dying. He said he loved being able to place his hands on his grandmother's back and give her Reiki. He said it felt really loving. Dave felt his Grandmother enjoyed the Reiki energy and, the love that flowed from it. What a beautiful Gift to be able to use Reiki to help someone when it's their time to cross over into another realm.

About Reiki Symbols

Symbols are used to help you connect and focus the Ki energy. The more you do Reiki the more you may find you use the symbols in more subtle ways. I have used Reiki symbols in different ways over the years. Sometimes I draw symbols on a person's body or, I imagine them in my mind.

Other times I may say the symbol's name in my mind. Trust your gut feelings and intuition as these feelings will guide you to what's best for the receiver. Remember the receiver may be yourself, a family member, an animal, a plant or a space! When you first learn Reiki you will use the symbols in ways to help you channel the Reiki and activate its energy. This will help you to attune to the healing power of Reiki.

Traditionally, Reiki Masters believed that the symbols were sacred and should be kept secret. These days Reiki symbols are seen on the internet and are published in books as knowledge has become more expansive and is shared more now.

Reiki courses used to cost thousands of dollars to do but nowadays they are more affordable.

Your Own Symbols

You can also use your own symbols in healing. A symbol is a vibration of energy. Draw your own symbols or imagine them. Use colours or sound vibrations. Be creative, as healing comes from universal energy, which is pure, creative and dynamic.

Symbols can be creative. Have your client draw a shape on a piece of paper. They may have their eyes open or closed when they draw. Say a healing prayer or meditation beforehand such as "we ask the spirit of this Divine Being to draw a symbol/sign that it needs right now." Put the symbol over their body or, under the massage table, to allow the Divine healing energy to work with it.

Symbols

Symbols can be visualised in your mind. Ask the symbol to show you a colour and watch as it is taken to where it needs to go in the person's body and chakras.

Symbols can be:

- Drawn on the roof of the mouth with your tongue.

- Drawn on a wall, with a pencil, before being painted over. My painter asked what I was doing one day. I told him I was drawing healing symbols on my wall to bless and cleanse the energy in the home. He said to me that it was a great idea as he was recovering from prostate cancer and he hoped he would benefit from the symbol's energies.

- Done with both hands held with palms together (as in the prayer/ namaste position) to clear rooms and to heal self and others.

- Thoughts – Say the name of the symbol in your mind and trust that the universe will direct the symbol to where it needs to go. Imagine a large symbol spread over the client's body and aura. Or, imagine a symbol engraved into every cell in their body.

- Requested – Ask what symbol you need now. Open your mind to sensing what symbol it is. You may receive the impression via an image, a feeling or a knowingness.

CHO KU REI

Figure 14.1

Means: Focus or Power

Cho Ku Rei is pronounced choke u ray.

- It represents the **on** button. It turns on the energy or power of Reiki.

- This symbol also enhances Reiki energy and calls it in.

- Cho Ku Rei is great for recharging, rejuvenating and healing on all levels of your Being.

- Think of Cho Ku Rei as a light switch that flicks on the energy and allows it to flow and channel through you.

- This symbol usually has an anticlockwise spiral but some people like using it in the other direction. Do what feels best for you.

- Cho Ku Rei is used to clear rooms as well as cleanse crystals.

- It is used over food and water to help the vibration and energy of these foods and to give a blessing of thanks and gratitude to the food/drink. Ask that your body digests and accepts it well. I have a colleague who travels regularly around the world for work. She often uses Reiki before she eats or drinks to help the atoms and molecules in the food and, to pray that they will be digested well by her body. Sometimes she cups her hand around a glass or, over a plate of food to send Reiki into the food. Other times she may just imagine the symbols in the food.

- You can also imagine (as thoughts are real) that Cho Ku Rei is over the shower head so that the water from the shower is filled with the healing power of Reiki. This will help the water's vibration (as everything is energy) so that it washes your body with tranquil and cleansing energy. You can also do this with your bath water.

- This symbol helps in manifesting your goals. Activate Cho Ku Rei to manifest your goals and dreams and ask that the best outcome be achieved. Trust that whatever happens in your future is for your Highest Good.

- I like to cleanse a room or space with Cho Ku Rei by visualising it in the corners of the room I am in. Also this symbol is effective in work spaces or areas that feel like the energy is dense and it needs an energetic shift. It's also lovely and empowering to say a quiet prayer, or affirmation while cleansing spaces. Ask that the room be filled with love, compassion and peace.

- Cho Ku Rei is also a protective symbol that will draw positive energies to you.
- Cho Ku Rei can be used in many ways so get inspired and use this limitless, amazing energy in many situations!

SEI HE KI

Figure 14.2

Means: Harmony, Emotional and Mental Healing.

Sei He Ki is pronounced say he key.

- Sei He Ki is used to help emotional and mental healing.
- It is used in healing addictions and habits.
- Works on the subconscious and assists in re-programming your mind so you can attain new healthier habits.
- Sei He Ki enhances harmony and rebalances the chakras.
- This symbol is linked with the moon and emotions that's why it's wonderful for emotional and mental healing.
- Sei He Ki helps in relationships, heals trauma and resolves conflict.
- Also helps heal negative thought patterns and creates more purpose in your life.
- This symbol helps with emotions such as fear, anger and grief.

Note: Emotions are messages for us to listen to and understand. Emotions are helpful if we learn to tap into why they are there. Releasing emotions through ways such as crying helps transform the energy so it will not stay locked and suppressed in our bodies. Emotion

= energy in motion. Emotions are meant to flow and be processed. They are a gift for us to listen to, to heal, to learn from. Emotions are you. They are that deep spiritual part of you that reveals what's going on inside you at a deep and profound level. Are you listening to your emotions or covering them up with food, anger, frustration and self-hate? Shine a light on your emotions. Honour them and make peace with them. Emotions can be scary sometimes. They can be strong and powerful. They can wake us up to make good changes in our life, thoughts and behaviours.

- The Sei He Ki symbol is also a form of psychic protection. If you feel others are annoying you or, getting in your aura or head space, use it. I find the best way to deal with this is to pray (ask/intend/ affirm) for the person and send them love and then send yourself love.

- Use this symbol when taking tests or exams to help calm your nerves and give you more confidence.

Exercise: Healing with Symbols

1. Sit or lie down, breathe deeply to relax and calm yourself. Imagine white gold light filling your body and the space around you.

2. Imagine the symbol/s going into your crown chakra, at the top of your head.

3. Affirm/pray for what your intention is, e.g. "I ask for healing around ... I hope that the best outcome is reached for all concerned." Or, "I am feeling ... could you give me insight into why this is happening?"

Usually within three days there will be a message of some sort given to you whether it's in a dream, words, a song you hear or, some other way that the cosmos will attempt to communicate an answer to you.

Ask that the energy stays with you for however long it is needed.

HON SHA ZE SHO NEN

Meaning: Distance and Remote Healing.

It is pronounced hon shar zay show nen.

Figure 14.3

- Hon sha ze sho nen is used to heal issues from your past, as well as past life issues.

- You can even use this symbol to send Reiki to someone overseas as the energy will still go there.

- This symbol will add an extra dimension and element to your healing. It will heal your past, present and future. Activate it and ask the energy to contribute to your healing sessions.

- Many years ago, when I first learnt Reiki 1, the teacher showed us the Hon sha ze sho nen symbol by projecting it up on a wall. We spent a long time practising how to draw this long and intricate symbol. I struggled to remember the detail in the symbol so one day I decided I would just say its name and trust that the powerful and loving universe would understand and know what I meant. I see the symbols image in my mind's eye when I use it. I tap into its energy, bond with it and ask it for assistance.

- Hon sha ze sho nen is great when used with Cho Ku Rei and Sei Hei Ki symbols. They all work well together as a trio of symbols.

Using the HON SHA ZE SHO NEN

You can do distance healing by imagining a mini person in-between your hands. Or you can write the person's name on a piece of paper

183

and hold that piece of paper and send Reiki that way. You can also visualise the person in front of you and send distance healing to them that way as well.

Exercise: Symbols Meditation

It is wonderful to meditate on the energy of the symbols. Take note of what happens in your meditations when using the different symbols.

Some people draw the symbol on paper and then hold it on their hands. Others place the symbol on their body or on a healing grid.

1. Close your eyes, breathe deeply several times to relax you and open up your intuitive senses.
2. Choose a symbol. You may like to draw or imagine your own symbol or energy.
3. Ask the symbol to show you a sound, vibration, colour, etc.
4. Ask this symbol to communicate and interact with you.
5. Ask the symbol to open up your heart and senses.
6. Now ask the symbol to go to where is needed in your body/life.
7. Relax and be still, let go and just be.

Laser Beam

Laser Beam is when you direct healing energy from a part of your body. Healing energy can be sent from your eyes, heart or hands. I have used the Laser Beam by visualising beams of healing energy going into a room, plant, person or around the earth. I also like to hold up my hand and allow a beam of energy to project from my palm onto something or someone else.

If tension is building between you and another person you can send a laser beam of energy to the other person or space, so that the energy in the area can be recalibrated. Also healing energy can be sent from the eyes, with love. I sent healing laser beams of healing energy to my friend Kat who went to work unwell one day. She did not know. I knew that on a deep soul level if she did not require the healing that it would be transferred somewhere else as the cosmos is all knowing and has infinite power and wisdom. I saw Kat after her work day and she said how her energy had increased during the day and how much better she had felt! Imagine being able to transform a situation by your love and healing wishes. Remember energy cannot be destroyed. It only can be transformed.

Ball of Light

This idea came to me one day and I find it's very effective. You imagine a ball of colourful light and place symbols into it. Use whatever symbols, or colours, you feel drawn to. They may be Reiki symbols or other symbols that feel powerful to you. Ask the ball to travel into your body and send healing to where it needs to go to.

You can send the healing ball of light to a country, a person or an issue. Use the ball of light to travel through a person's body and watch where it goes to. Your ball of symbols has inner wisdom and will know where it needs to go. You can also send the healing ball of light to heal, cleanse and rejuvenate a problem knowing that the Divine Love of the cosmos will send its healing rays to the situation.

Anna's Reiki Symbols

I remember using healing symbols the day before I went to a radio program to be interviewed. I was at home doing self-hypnosis and imagining that I would feel relaxed and that I would express myself well in the interview.

I called in my Guides and Higher Self and sent healing energy to the radio station space to help prepare me for the interview.

I asked what symbol I needed and I was shown the Hon Sha Ze Sho Nen distance healing symbol. I also saw the Cho Ku Rei and I added in the Sei He Ki too. I saw a vision of the symbols in colours. The Sei He Ki was a brilliant blue colour, the Cho Ku Rei was golden yellow and the Hon Sha Ze Sho Nen was a blue/black colour.

The radio interview went better than I expected. Thank you symbols!

Reiki Attunements

Reiki attunements occur when symbols and energy are transferred to the student by the Reiki Master teacher during an attunement ritual. This attunement process opens the crown, heart, and palm chakras and prepares the student to channel Reiki. The Reiki attunement is a beautiful spiritual experience.

The attunement energies are channelled into the student through the Reiki Master teacher. Reiki guides and other spiritual beings help with the ritual. Some students have had mystical experiences, after an attunement, such as receiving personal messages, tingles, a healing, visions or a past life memory.

People may find an increase in psychic ability and intuition in the months after doing a Reiki course. Attunements are like a powerful activation. I love giving attunement ceremonies as I find them deeply sacred.

Energy Blocks and Disease

Emotional blocks can cause disease and illness that's why it's great to be aware of your feelings, thoughts and actions as the more aligned we are the better your energy will flow and the more energy and vitality your body will feel.

Exercise: Group Healing

1. One person lies on the massage table and healers stand around the table. Each person lays their hand on a certain area of the person's body for about 5–10 minutes.

2. After about 5–10 minutes a swap occurs where one of the other healers will lie on the table to receive healing. Continue swapping until everyone gets a turn.

This is a wonderful sacred experience as everyone is able to give and receive.

At one of my healing courses we had one person lie on the massage table while the others placed themselves around the table. We placed our hands on an area of the body e.g. someone would have their hands on the person's head, another on the feet area, while another laid hands on the person's back. We would all close our eyes, relax and draw symbols in our mind or, on roof of our mouths. We would say a short prayer or intention. We would swap over after 5 minutes, so each person had a turn on the table. It was really effective and different people felt different levels of heat, cold or energy flowing through to them. Group Healing is a wonderful and nurturing experience.

Scanning

You can scan the body by sending beams of light over and around the person. Look inside, or around the body for any changes, colours or images. Open up your third eye to scan around the aura and body. You may see colours or images around the body, organs or chakras.

If I am scanning the body and am shown a number 8, for example, I may ask the person what happened around age eight as the superconscious has shown me something that needs to be addressed. Some people do not have memories of what happened at certain ages and that is OK as the subconscious remembers and, Reiki or laying on hands, will naturally heal on this subconscious level.

Grounding with Energy

I used to feel light headed and dizzy when I did not have enough good quality foods to ground me and keep my energy stable. Foods like junk food, sugar, wheat, alcohol and coffee are not always good at keeping the body grounded and balanced. Nuts, fruit, vegetables and other good quality foods, help to nourish the bones, muscles and brain so that you will feel more centred, vibrant and connected to self and others. The more grounded I am the better I can serve myself and others.

Other good ways to ground your energy, and spirit, is to be in nature and earthing. Take your shoes off and feel the earth beneath your feet. Activities like gardening or walking are good for your energy as they help in healing self and others. Nature recharges your energy battery and revitalises your cells and your aura. Place your palms on the earth to activate your 11th chakra and to allow cleansing energy to come into your body.

Research[27] on earthing shows that being outside barefoot helps stress, pain, inflammation, sleep, heart disease and other health issues. Earthing is as important to humans as exercise, sunshine, air, water and good food!

Healing Crystal Grid

Healing crystal grids are fabulous to do as they activate the healing energy. Grids are like patterns or designs that you create. You can intuitively place crystals in a way that feels right to you. Some people make crystal grids into shapes such as a triangle, circle or square patterns. Others people add in oracle cards, photos, flowers and words

27 https://www.ncbi.nlm.nih.gov/pmc/articles/PMC3265077/

to make their healing crystal grids amazing! Place the crystals and objects in a way that inspires you. You will be surprised by what you create. I love adding a few candles or tea lights, around the grid to add an element of sacredness and divinity to it. You can also put your crystals, or stones, into the shape of a Reiki symbol.

Ask the healing energy to activate your grid for however long you require. Pray and ask for healing in whatever area in your life you need. You can also send distance healing to family members or, the world in general if you wish. You may like to add to the grid any drawings, symbols, words or hopes you may have. The grid will continuously send healing as it is linked to the power of the universe. Reiki activates this Divine Universal power that we can tap into if we command it to. You can even just imagine a healing crystal grid for protection, energy and support. You'll be able to feel the divine energy that comes through your grid.

Cassandra's Healing

Cassandra contacted me for a reading. Cassandra was a nurse in her late 30s and her aim for the session was to help with self-sabotage, beliefs and low self-esteem.

Cassandra settled into my office and nervously smiled at me. I sensed straight away that this session would go quite deep. Cassandra was ready to find the core truth about what was happening in her life. She was upset that she was childless and alone. Cassandra had been attracting partners that she felt were wrong for her. She would meet them, fix them then dump them.

"Same story, different guy" she perceptively remarked.

I clairvoyantly saw a baby girl in her aura and she confirmed she had been pregnant in the past. I also saw a male in spirit on her father's side. In my mind, I asked this spirit how they died. I was shown some dark-coloured intestines so I mentioned the relative died of something to do with the intestines.

Cassandra affirmed they had died of bowel cancer. I was also shown a wedding dress but the bottom of the white wedding dress was black representing her broken engagement.

I did a tarot card reading for Cassandra, but before this we had a chat about her life. I asked what she wanted in life and what were her goals. Without hesitation Cassandra said she wanted love, acceptance and children. She was unhappy in her work life and felt like she gave her all yet didn't get back what she felt she deserved.

Cassandra lay on the healing table as I began Reiki on her.

I asked Cassandra what happened at age 13. The guides/super-conscious often give numbers if they want us to address a certain time period in a person's life. Cassandra wasn't sure what happened at age 13 so I decided to ask her heart for answers.

I asked her to close her eyes. I also asked her to breathe deeply to slow down the beta brain so that she could drop into relaxing alpha brainwaves. I asked the superconscious for information around age 13 and I could see a girl wearing a school uniform. I told Cassandra what I saw. This triggered information and she started crying. She recalled an incident where she was bullied by a group of guys when she walked home from school. It was so traumatic for her that part of her shutdown that day. She lost interest in school and became uninterested in life.

I then asked her to imagine golden light around the boys involved, so the subconscious would see the situation as healed, to let go and not keep recreating negative patterns of behaviour. She often felt like a victim so we wanted to change her internal programming to feel more empowered about her future and being able to strive forward in life.

Cassandra cut negative cords between herself and the boys. I asked her current 36-year-old self to express what she would say to the boys. She said she would tell the boys to go away and not to pick on people.

I asked her heart to take herself to another time where she needed healing. I saw age six appear and asked her to recall anything that may have happened around age 6. Meanwhile I asked for more information from the higher realms and heard the word "brother."

Cassandra told me her brother also picked on her a lot when she was around age 6. I took Cassandra into a beautiful meditation to help heal the 6-year-old within her. Cassandra released a lot of tears in this session which was really healing for her soul.

Healing Protocol

I remember when a symbol appeared to me several years ago. I began my autumn walk by heading towards the grassy hill near my home. Walking is calming and cleansing for my Spirit. Being in nature gives me a refreshing break from my home office. On my walks, I love looking at the clouds, hearing the bird sounds and smelling the fragrant flowers. After my serene walk I returned home and decided to meditate on my trampoline. I closed my eyes and was amazed to see, in my mind's eye, a maroon and blue symbol. I drew the image down and this symbol became the symbol for the course I designed, and teach, called Psychic Reiki.

Below is information that I teach to the Psychic Reiki students. It's a beautiful process that I have seen work brilliantly over and over again.

Like all good things, it can be adapted to suit your needs. As always tune into your heart, as your heart is linked to spirit energy and has the answers for you.

Enjoy!

Psychic Reiki Healing Protocol

You may need pillows, sheet, blanket, music, crystals, candles, water.

PREPARATION:

BREATHE deeply into belly (x10)
to activate alpha brainwaves and open up chakras as well.

PROTECT self & room with Golden/White bright light.

CALL (x3) Guides in & spiritual team, that love us unconditionally, to support you and your client.

SAY a Prayer/ Affirmation.

ASK Client: Why are you here today? What's your aim for today's session?

LOOK and sense their aura, chakras and Spirit Guide.

EXPLAIN briefly what happens in a Reiki healing session. Check if it's OK to lay hands on their body. Is touching the feet OK?

Lie client facing up or down. (Or on a chair/bed or another relaxed position.)

Do SPIRAL pattern gently on back (use your intuition) or use a figure 8 motion. Do REIKI HAND positions by using your hands together side by side or using them apart. You can also use your fingertips.

Use REIKI SYMBOLS in your mind; on roof of mouth or draw over the body.

ASK the person to take deep slow breaths and say positive words to them. Sense their energy/aura/chakras.

Once they are comfortable you can start on the healing. Always remember when doing Reiki or, any hands-on healing, to touch the client appropriately and with respect.

You can complete Part 1 Healing and Part 2 Visualisation together or separately depending on what is comfortable for you and your client.

PART 1: HEALING:

TURN person over (or if in chair move position) if you wish.

ASK " How does your _____ (or, this situation _____) make you feel?"

Example 1 **Question:** How does your sore back make you feel? **Answer:** I feel irritable/annoyed.

Example 2 **Question:** How does your boss make you feel?
Answer: I feel insecure/unworthy.

ASK Take yourself back to a time you felt those emotions. Allow an image or memory to come to you.

Jog their memory by saying What age were you? What happened? Who was there? Remind them to relax and breathe.

ASK "What was the lesson, or insight, for you?" Get them to imagine these past events as healed with golden white light.

PART 2: VISUALISATION:

Invite the person to relax as you take them on a visualisation. Describe a magical, natural sanctuary that they go to. Allow the visions to come to you or make up your own visualisation. Use words that describe the natural environment such as the smells, sounds, colours, etc.

Guide the person to go to a Garden. In the garden they will meet their Guide. Ask this Guide to give any advice or messages. The Guide will share this advice and messages via a symbol, feeling, image, sound, colour, or just a knowingness. Now walk further down the path, see the success bridge. As they walk over the bridge they land on the other side of the bridge and see themselves living in abundance, success, health and good fortune.

To **END** the session: Hold feet: ground and centre the person. Imagine a WATERFALL cascading over both of you cleansing the room. Thank the Guides & Energy.

WATER should be offered after the healing and remind your client to keep hydrated over the next few days. If they get loose bowels next day this just means emotional energy and clearing has released through their body and chakras.

TELL the client to "Go gently" in the next few days. They can journal their emotions if they like. Refer client to other modalities if you feel they may need further support.

TOUCH the earth or have a sea salt/epsom bath to cleanse your aura and relax yourself.

"When you touch others, touch them with all the love, care and compassion that you can find within yourself."[28]

Lana – From Cancer to Health

Lana was a client who I will never forget. Her story inspired me and it highlighted to me the immense power that healing brings to one's soul.

Lana arrived at my clinic one winter's day. She was 52-years old and had a large blended family with her second husband Joel. Lana was recovering from Breast cancer and chemotherapy treatment. Mentally Lana was still struggling with the aftermath of her cancer diagnosis.

"I'm angry that I'm angry," she spat out. "I'm usually happy but now I'm grumpy and sad. Is this all there is to life?" I nodded and listened quietly.

Lana continued. "I can't remember things, I'm usually a glass ½ full type of person but I feel ungrateful."

28 Chia, M. & Chia, M. (1990) *Internal Organs Chi Massage* (p.7), Healing Tao Books, NY.

I asked Lana about her feelings towards the cancer. Lana revealed that when she initially had an ultrasound she was shown a 3cm mass in her breast. She'd seen on the screen an image of a " black mass of tendrils." This image haunted her. It was "just evil," she said.

Lana had never had Reiki before but she was keen to experience it. I saw Lana several times in the next few months. In each session, we did Reiki, shamanic and crystal healing. Lana loved hands-on healing and would remark that my hands felt hot.

In each session we delved more into her emotions and her past. We did visualisations where her subconscious transformed the evil black tendrils into a beautiful pink mass which evolved into a yellow butterfly! Healing helped her to gain back her inner power. She learnt how to meditate and do mantras.

At our last session, Lana was grateful and humbled for our time together. I was impressed by her willingness to grow, learn and love. Lana told me that she was back to her normal self or "new normal" as she called it.

She said her family was pleased to see her laughing again. She took more holidays. Lana relaxed more and became more at peace with her life.

This is what healing does. It changes lives and it changes families! When one person heals we all heal.

CHAPTER 15

Crystal Healing & Sacred Geometry

The word **crystal** covers many forms of gemstones and minerals. Throughout history crystals have been used as sacred objects for ceremonies, meditation, clarity and to help with healing. Crystals are used in computers, lasers and other technology.

Crystals come in different sizes, shapes and colours depending on where they are found. Many crystals come from the earth but some come from space such as meteorites. Some crystals are synthetically produced and others are artificially coloured so you may want to check this when you purchase them. In jewellery shops the gems that are not real are called "created." Real crystals have their own individual frequency. When you hold a crystal you may be able to feel the vibration of the crystal's energies.

How do Crystals Work?

Crystals have electrical properties, and it's the piezoelectric property of a small quartz crystal that gives a quartz watch its accuracy. Crystals are also used in ultrasound equipment and even microphones!

Scientists define a crystal as "the regular, repeating arrangement of atoms in a solid. The atoms are essentially fixed in place but can vibrate slightly."[29]

What is piezoelectricity?

Interestingly, the piezoelectric effect was discovered in 1880 by two French physicists, brothers Pierre and Paul Curie. They found the piezoelectric effect in the crystals quartz and tourmaline. They used the Greek work piezein, which means "to press."[30] The piezoelectric effect is electromagnetic so it can affect our energy, aura, thoughts and cells.

Piezoelectricity is when you "squeeze" a crystal to get it to produce a voltage. Also, some crystals will vibrate when electricity is passed through them. Some crystals even become a type of battery with positive and negative charges.

There is a theory that the electrical energy from our bodies can cause the crystals to vibrate and give off energy and vice versa.

Crystals Types

Crystals come in many shapes and sizes. They can be tumbled, cut and polished, and made into shapes such as spheres, eggs, pyramids and wands.

---

29 http://www.explainthatstuff.com/piezoelectricity.html
30 http://www.explainthatstuff.com/piezoelectricity.html

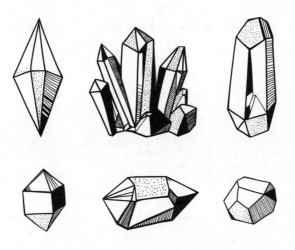

Figure 15.1

Double Terminators

These crystals have a point at each end which allows energy in and out of the crystal.

Single Terminated Wands

Have a single point at one end. The other end may be rounded or uneven. Single terminated wands are used in healing or meditation as well as to cleanse.

Single Point or Generator

Have approximately six sides that come to a point at one end. The point helps focus the energy.

Polished (made) Generators

Polishing and shaping of the points allows the energy to flow well.

Crystal Wands

Some people use the smooth end for gentle massaging.

Pyramids

Make superb room and meditation pieces.

Balls

Great for gazing or scrying. Good for psychic readings too.

Eggs

Traditional Chinese shape which is said to represent our inner self & essence. They can also be called fertility eggs.

Hearts

Symbolise love and helps strengthen your own heart both emotionally & physically.

Slices

Larger stones may be cut into slices to show their inner beauty.

Caves and Geodes

Good for cleansing and charging other crystals or items. I find these are great communicators and once you start talking to them they will link into your energy. You may feel vibrations and a connection to the crystal.

Chunks

Chunks are crystals without sides. They are more like a lump or mass of crystals. They help build up energy in a room or can be used for meditating. Crystal chunks can be placed near a computer to help rebalance the electrical energy from it. I have an amethyst chunk near my laptop that helps me when I am typing.

Clusters

Clusters are also like a chunk yet you can see more defined crystals in a cluster. A cluster looks like a group of crystals that has formed and grown together. The different crystals help to magnify the total energy of the cluster. Clusters are good also for energy, cleansing and healing. Clusters are fabulous for cleansing and recharging other crystals too.

Cut and Polished Crystals

These crystals come in shapes such as pyramids, wands or spheres. Each shape will hold a different frequency and vibe. Each person will connect with each crystal differently just like a person will respond to another person differently.

Tumble Stones

Tumble stones are stones, rocks or crystals that have been tumbled many times until they become smoother and polished. These stones are smallish and are usually reasonably priced. Sometimes people keep tumble stones in their pockets or handbags.

Choosing a Crystal

Follow your intuition and choose what feels right for you and what you are drawn to. If you are choosing a crystal for someone else just imagine that person in your mind and heart. Focus on the crystal and then tune into what that person would benefit from.

Holding a crystal in your hand will allow you to tune into its vibration and energy.

Be aware of your gut feelings when buying crystals. When buying a crystal you may like to hold the crystal and feel the effect it has on your body. How does it make you feel? Do you feel calm and centred? Does your body tingle? I once spotted a purple amethyst and pink *rhodochrosite* pendant in a crystal shop. I asked a lady to open up the crystal cabinet. I held the pendant and immediately started crying as it connected with my heart and soul. It had a powerful effect on me.

There are wholesale places that sell crystals at good prices. There are also some online if you wish to google them. They allow you to buy wholesale if you join up with their company. Some places need you to prove that you are buying crystals to sell, make or use for teaching.

Cleansing Your Crystals

Some ways to cleanse your crystals are:

- **Water** – Wash them in running water. Please be aware some crystals deteriorate in water so it's best to be careful when using any liquids to cleanse crystals.

- **Breath/Chi** – Use your chi or life force energy. To do this, take your crystal and blow into the crystal.

  Alternatively, take a deep breath, imagine yourself filled with brilliant clear white light, and then blow through, or across the crystal. Imagine a Reiki symbol over the crystal as you do this. The American Indians were said to have cleansed their crystals with a short breath. If I hold a crystal while reading for a client I will blow air onto it as a way to cleanse and revitalise the crystal's energy.

- **On other Crystals** – Place the crystal on a crystal cluster or in a geode as these will help the crystal to cleanse.

- **Carnelian** – Keep a carnelian crystal with your other crystals as a carnelian helps clean and cleanse crystals.

- **Sea Salt** – Sea salt is very cleansing. You can place your crystals in a bowl of dry sea salt after using them. The bowl of salt can be replaced every few weeks or, when you intuitively get a feeling that it's time to do it.

- **Colour** – I have a clear quartz cluster and when I ask what does it need for cleansing, I'm shown a pink colour. I then imagine pink colour around the clear quartz. Crystals respond to our energies, our thoughts and our motivations. Connect with them as you'll be surprised how they communicate with you.

- **Sunlight** – The sun can clear and purify energy in your crystal. Remember though that the sun can fade some crystals so use a clock timer so you remember how long the crystal has been out-side in the sun or, on your windowsill.

- **Moonlight** – Many people use Moon light to cleanse and rejuvenate their crystals. The full moon is a favourite time people use as the energies are higher around a full moon.

- **Earth** – Place a crystal on a pot plant or, on the ground outdoors. This is a fabulous way to cleanse and recharge a crystal's energies and vibrations.

- **Music** – Playing beautiful music will help the crystals to cleanse and rebalance.

- **Incense** – You can smudge your crystals with incense to cleanse them as well.

- **Ask** – I was teaching a Crystal healing course one weekend. I had finished using a crystal and I asked the crystal, telepathically, how it would like to be cleansed. I could see a mini waterfall above the crystal. But, before I gave the answer, I asked the class what did they think the crystal needed. One lady in the group exclaimed, "Oh I see a waterfall running through the crystal so it wants water to cleanse it." I imagined, in my mind, a waterfall above the crystal. This cleansed and rebalanced the crystal just like it told me. Ask the Crystal what it needs to be cleansed, open your 3rd eye, and your other clairs, and see what comes to you. Magic!

MOHS : Mineral Hardness Scale

To learn more deeply about crystals it's important to know about the MOHS Mineral Hardness Scale. The MOHS scale measures the hardness of a mineral by its resistance to scratching. The MOHS grid shows minerals from softest to hardest.

Who developed the MOHS scale?

Friedrich Mohs developed the MOHS scale in 1812. He was an Austrian/German mineralogist.

Table 15.1 MOHS Grid

MOHS				
Mohs Hardness	Mineral or Substance	Absolute Hardness	Scratch Test	Other minerals
1.0 (softest)	Talc (Found in Talcum powder)	1	Scrapeable with fingernail	Soapstone
3.0	Calcite	9	Scratch with copper	Pearl, copper
4.0	Fluorite	21	Scratch with a nail	Malachite, iron
5.0	Apatite	48	Scratch with a nail	Cobalt, tooth enamel
7.0	Quartz	100	Scratches window glass	Tourmaline, Adventurine
8.0	Topaz	200	Scratches glass and quartz	Cubic Zirconia
10.0 (hardest)	Diamond	1600	Hardest as unable to be scratched	

Crystals Geometric Shapes:

Crystals have internal structures made from geometric patterns. Judy Hall[31] highlights that even though a crystal may look a certain way on the outside the inside of the crystal will have one of 8 patterns (Refer to Table 15.2).

Table 15.2

Shape	Meaning	Shape	Meaning
Hexagonal	Made from hexagons. This shape helps balance energy and create healing.	Orthorhombic	Made from rhomboids. These are good for clearing and cleansing.
Cubic	Made from squares. These crystals are grounding, stable and create peace. **Note:** This is the only shape that does not bend the light rays as the light just goes right through it.	Triclinic	Made from trapeziums. They absorb energy and help link with other dimensions.
Trigonal	Made from triangles. These crystals revitalise and shield the aura.	Monoclinic	Made from parallelograms. This shape helps to purify and give insight.
Tetragonal	Made from rectangles. These crystals absorb and transmute energy.	Amorphous	No inner shapes so energy passes through quite quickly & effectively. Helps with changes.

---

31 Hall, J. 2013. *The Encyclopedia of Crystals*, Octopus, UK.

Anna's Crystal A-Z Chart

On the following pages is a chart[32] I put together as a guide for you. I studied biochemistry in my Health Science degree so I love learning about the chemical components of crystals. I hope you enjoy the fascinating information about crystals and what they are made of. I designed the chart below for easy access so you can learn about crystals and their uniqueness. I enjoy referring to the chart when I want to know more about the structure and composition of crystals.

---

32 Hall, J. 2013. *The Encyclopedia of Crystals*, Octopus, UK.

Table 15.3

CRYSTAL Chemistry	Colour (colours vary)	Benefits	Crystal System that it's made of	Hardness	Affects Chakra	Places it's found
Ammolite (Calcium carbonate with impurities)	Browns	A Holy stone. Attracts prosperity. Aids in clarity and flow of life. Heals karma and represents the cycle of life.	Fossil	4	6th, 7th	Canada, Morocco or an imitation
Auralite 23 (Silicon dioxide plus many more)	Multicolours	Pastlife, Shamanic healing, Akashic records and Generational healing. Helps to bring the best out of other crystals.	Trigonal	7	All	Canada
Aventurine (Silicon dioxide)	Greens	Harmonises and protects the heart chakra. Is known as the Stone of Opportunity.	Trigonal	7	3rd, 4th	Various
Amazonite (Potassium aluminum silicate + copper)	Green-blue	Protects from electromagnetic energy. Helps grief as well as useful for negotiating. Great for musician and writers.	Triclinic	6– 6.5	3,4,5	Various
Amethyst (Silicon dioxide with iron)	Purple	Turns negativity into love. Is good for scrying, dreaming and protects from geopathic stress. Helps with change.	Trigonal	7	6,7,8,9	Various

Name (composition)	Colour	Description	Crystal system	Hardness	Chakra	Location
Amber (Carbon, Hydrogen, Oxygen)	Orange	Amber is fossilised tree resin. Grounds, heals and protects. Turns negative energy into positive energy.	Non-crystalline	2–2.5	5th	Various
Ametrine (Silicon dioxide with iron)	Is a mixture of Amethyst and Citrine so colour is yellow & purple.	Protects against Psychic Attack. It releases toxins and stuck issues. Helps energy, meditation and brings positive change to one's life. Great for journeying.	Trigonal	7	3rd, 6th	Various
Angelite (Calcium Sulphate)	Blue	Comes from Celestite. Connects to Higher realms. Helps understanding of Astrology. Improves telepathic communication.	Orthorhombic	3.5	5th, 6th	Peru
Apache Tear (Silicon dioxide with impurities)	Black	Heals sadness and grief. Is linked to Obsidian. Helps forgiveness. Shields the aura. Detoxes also.	Amorphous	5-5.5	1st,3rd	Mexico
Apophyllite (Hydrous Calcium, potassium silicate)	Colourless, white, grey, green, brown	"Apo" means off & "phyllon" means leaf in Greek. Carries Akashic Records. Great for healing. Connects with devas, fairies and plant energy.	Tetragonal	4.5-5	6th, 7th	Various

Aquamarine (Beryllium, Aluminium, Silicon, oxygen+Iron)	Green-blue	Stone of the Sea Goddess. Boosts clarity and changes old patterns. A Humanitarian stone. Useful in meditation.	Hexagonal	7.5–8	All. Opens 3rd eye.	Various
Azurite (Carbon, Hydrogen, Oxygen+copper)	Blue-indigo	The copper helps the nervous system. Useful for Channelling. Helps reprogram cells in the body. Boosts metaphysical abilities.	Monoclinic	3.5–4	6,7,8	Various
Bloodstone (silicon dioxide)	Deep green with red streaks	Bloodstone healing stone of rebirth. Helps sleep. Re-energises and heals. Allows one to live in the present moment.	Trigonal	7	1,2,3,4	Various
Blue Lace Agate (silicon dioxide)	Blue with white streaks and gold flecks	Blue Lace Agate is a stone of peace as it reduces anger and eradicates negative programming. Also helps soul with fear of rejection and brings in pure truth.	Trigonal	6	5,6,7	Various
Calcite (Calcium carbonate)	Various	Calcite means lime in Greek. A great stone for hope. Boosts memory and creates emotional balance. Cleanses the environment and focuses the mind.	Hexagonal	3	Depends on colour	Various

Stone	Colour	Description	Crystal system	Hardness	Chakra	Zodiac
Carnelian (Silicon dioxide, Iron)	Orange-red	Carnelian is the stone of hope, courage and strength. Is able to clean other stones.	Trigonal	7	Base, Sacral	Various
Celestite (Strontium sulfate)	Blue	Celestite is a stone that has a high vibration. A Magical & intuitive stone. Heals the aura and helps with public speaking.	Orthorhombic	3–3.5	5,6,7,8	Various
Chrysotile (Magnesium Iron Silicate Hydroxide)	Green	Releases the past. Links to your power animal. Is toxic so use as a tumbled stone.	Monoclinic	2.5–4	3rd Eye	Various
Chrysocolla (Copper, Aluminum, silicon, hydrogen)	Blue	Chrysocolla helps be present. Heals heart and emotions. Great cleanser for the aura and houses.	Orthorhombic	2–4	All	Various
Chrysoprase (Silicon dioxide and nickel)	Green	Chrysoprase is the stone of optimism, acceptance and inner-child healing. Helps with forgiveness. Creates deep states of meditation.	Trigonal	7	Heart, sacral	Various
Citrine (Silicon dioxide)	Yellow-golden	Citrine is a wealth stone. It is a powerful cleanser and recharges the energy field.	Trigonal	7	All	Various

Dalmatian Stone (Sodium, Iron, Magnesium, Silicate Hydroxide)	White with small black dots (like a Dalmatian dog!)	Dalmatian Stone moves energy from head to heart. Creates fun & playful energy. Changes patterns so you can move forward in life.	Monoclinic	5–7.5	3,4,5	Mexico
Diamond (made from carbon with impurities)	White	Does not need to be recharged. Heals auras. Is a symbol of love and abundance.	Cubic	10	7th	Various
Emerald (Beryllium, Aluminium, Silicon)	Green	Emerald is the stone of patience, loyalty, unity, partnership. Helps success in relationships.	Hexagonal	7.5–8	4th	Various
Fluorite (Calcium, fluoride)	Green-purple colour	Fluorite helps memory and concentration. Creates order and clears electromagnetic stress.	Cubic	4	4th	Various
Fuchsite (potassium, aluminum, silicate mineral)	Green	Helps with clingy relationships, addictions and low self-esteem. Helps with channelling information. Heals past lives. Gives inner strength & stability.	Monoclinic	2–3.5	8th	Various

Garnet (Magnesium, aluminium silicate)	Dark red	Is good for libido, passion, vitality and energy. A very energising stone. Assists in tantra and kundalini energy. Heals sabotage patterns in subconscious. Linked to pituitary gland. May induce past life memories. Helps intensify other crystals.	Cubic	6–7.5	All	Various
Hematite (Iron oxide)	Silver, black	Grounds, protects, and helps with stress and mental powers. Links to subconscious. Made of iron so links with blood & our flow in life.	Hexagonal	5.5–6.5	1, 8, 10	Various
Howlite (calcium, borosilicate hydroxide)	White, grey	Howlite helps anger and insomnia. Drops your mask away. May link to past lives. Helps with achieving your goals.	Monoclinic	3.5	6th	USA
Jade (Sodium, aluminium silicate)	Green	Jade is a symbol of serenity, good luck and abundance in one's life. Protects children. Helps with dreams.	Monoclinic	6	6th	Various
Jasper (Silicon dioxide)	Various	Jasper is grounding and helps organs in the body. A shamanic stone which helps stress and is nurturing. Aids dream recall.	Trigonal	7	All	Various

Name (Composition)	Colour	Properties	Crystal System	Hardness	Chakra	Location
Kyanite (Aluminium silicate)	Grey, green-blue	Activates the higher chakras as it tunes into higher vibrations. Never needs cleaning. Links us to our Guides.	Triclinic	5.5–7	5th	Various
Labradorite (Calcium, Sodium, Silicon, Alumnium)	Grey, brown, greenish, blue	It increases telepathy and amplifies joy. Releases negativity and other people's energy hooks. Prevents energy leakage and enhances energy.	Triclinic	5–6	6, 7, 8	Various
Lapis Lazuli (Sodium, Calcium Aluminosilicate)	Royal Blue with *gold flecks* of pyrite	A royal stone. Great for hormones, migraines. It aids communication, thought, dreams and psychic ability. Encourages listening from the heart.	Cubic	5–6	5th, 6th, 7th	Various
Larimar (Sodium, Calcium, Silicon, hydrogen)	Blue-Green	Magnetises joy, peace and love to you. This stone helps one to go with the flow. Connects to earth energy as well.	Triclinic	5	3,4,5,6,7	Bahamas and Dominican Republic (Caribbean Region)
Lepidolite (Aluminium, lithium, potasssium, Silicate)	Lilac, grey, rose	Is wonderful to clear electromagnetic energy so place near computers and in offices. Links to cosmos & Akashic records. It may vibrate if put on the body. Contains lithium so aids mental stability.	Monoclinic	5	All	Various

	Colour	Properties	Crystal System	Hardness	Chakra	Location
Malachite (copper, hydrogen, carbon)	Green	A stone of change. Helps you to get out of your comfort zone. Protects against the evil eye, negative energy and electrosmog.	Monoclinic	3.4–4	1,2,3,4	Various
Moonstone (potassium, aluminum, silicate) Part of Feldspar group.	White, colourless, brown, grey	A stone of new beginnings. Connects with the moon and your emotional emotional self. Reminds you of the cycles of life. Enhance intuition and dreaming.	Monoclinic	6	3rd, 6th	India, Sri Lanka, Australia
Obsidian- (Silicon dioxide with impurities)	Black *Snowflake Obsidian- is black and has white patches on it which is feldspar.	Absorbs negativity and helps inner power, self-worth & self-esteem. Helps one to surrender and to see the Gifts in our mistakes. Creates clarity of mind. Clears past life issues and stuck trauma. Good to scry with. It grounds from base chakra to centre of earth.	Amorphous *Has no crystalline structure so works quickly. A powerful stone.	5–5.5	All.	Mexico, volcanic regions
Onyx (Silicon dioxide, Carbon, iron)	Black	Reduces stress and helps self control. Stone helps you to see the future. Holds memories so good to do psychometry with.	Trigonal	7	8th,9th	Various

Opal (Silica + impurities)	Colourless, white, yellow, red, orange, green, brown, black, blue, pink	Good for self-worth. A karmic stone that teaches what we put out there energetically magnetises our path to us. Choose carefully your behaviours so the magic of the Opal can draw to you the very best.	Amphorous	5.5–6.5	All	Various
Pearl (Calcium carbonate)	white, pink, silver, cream, brown, green, blue, black, yellow, and purple	Made inside the soft tissue of a living shelled mollusk or oyster. A gem that can be dissolved with vinegar. Pearl's message is not to let acidic foods and situations affect you. Rise above, heal and love the unlovable. Irritations in life can bring us great gifts. An astral stone that's linked to the moon.	Amphorous	2.5–4.5	All	Various
Peridot (Magnesium, Iron, Silicon, Oxygen)	Green	Peridot is also called olivine. Helps healers. A stone that helps release the past as well as toxins. Great for cleansing mind, body and soul.	Orthorhombic	6.5–7	3,4	Various
Petrified Wood (fossilised wood) Complex chemistry	Browns	Petrified Wood helps to ground and release past pain. Brings ancient wisdom. Heals generational healing and DNA. Akashic records.	Complex	8	All	Various

Name (Chemistry)	Colour	Description	Crystal System	Hardness	Chakra	Location
Prehnite (Hydrous calcium Aluminium)	Green - yellow	Prehnite is a stone of unconditional love and healing. Links you to the universes energy grid and Higher Beings.	Orthorhombic	6–6.5	6th	Various
Pyrite (Iron Sulfide)	brass – yellow	Called Fools gold because it looks like gold. Protects the aura and spirit. Helps confidence and self-esteem.	Cubic	6–6.5	All	Various
Quartz(silicon dioxide) *Smokey Quartz has aluminum/ lithium in it.	Various colours such as pink, golden, green and blue.	Quartz: Clear Quartz is the most powerful healing and energy amplifier. It can project energy. Also purifies people and other stones. Stores information so can be programmed.	Hexagonal	7	All	Worldwide
Rhodochrosite (Manganese carbonate)	Pink	Represents self love and compassion. Good for healing wounds & trauma. Heals sexual abuse. A truth stone.	Hexangonal	3.5–4	1, 3, 4,	Various
Rhodonite (Manganese, Silicon, oxygen, Calcium, Magnesium, Iron)	Pink and black	Pink is for love while black heals our blocks. A first aid stone that heals betrayal and abandonment. A stone of forgiveness.	Triclinic	5.5–6.5	3rd, 4th	Various

Ruby (Aluminium Oxygen)	Deep Red	Name is from latin word "ruber" which means red. Enhances your passion and motivation and. Stone of abundance.	Trigonal	9	1st, 4th	Various
Sapphire (Aluminium Oxide)	Blue	Sanskrit for Saturn. Helps with legal matters. Brings in Gifts. Helps with communication.	Hexagonal	9	5th	Various
Selenite (Hydrated calcium sulfate)	White	Selenite is used in meditation to bring peace and connection. A high vibration stone that protects homes. Helps the subconscious to heal. Calms & balances emotions.	Monoclinic	2	7th	Various
Shiva Lingam (Complex sandstone)	Browns	Represents God Shiva and Kali. Symbolises sexuality and male energy. Used in raising and healing kundalini energy. Release cords to old relationships. Helps with romance and allows new relationships to enter one's life.	Complex crystal system	1	1st	India – or artificially made.
Sodalite (Sodium, aluminium silicate, chloride)	Blue	Activates the third eye and pineal & pituitary glands. Brings clarity and emotional peace to families & groups. Message is to be true to self. Helps geopathic stress.	Cubic	5–5.6	5th	Various

Name (composition)	Colour	Properties	Crystal system	Hardness	Chakra	Location
Tigers Eye (Silicon dioxide with impurities)	Browns	Tigers Eye helps positivity and 3rd eye vision. Heals disorders and addictions.	Hexagonal	4–7	6th	Various
Tourmaline – Black (Complex silicate)	Black	It balances, protects and grounds. Can generate an electric charge. Good for scrying.	Trigonal	7–7.5	10th	Various
Topaz – clear (Aluminium Silicon, Hydrogen, Oxygen, Fluorine)	Colourless although some do have colours	Helps you tap into cosmic energies. Stone of purification.	Orthorhombic	8	7, 8, 9	Various
Turquoise (Aluminium, copper; phosphorous, hydrogen, oxygen)	Green-Blue	Turquoise is a calming stone. It helps with writing, communication, leadership and travel.	Triclinic	5–6	5th, 6th	Various
Unakite (Complex)	Green, coral, earth tones	Unakite is said to be a vision stone as it opens the third eye. It goes to the root cause of an disease. Helps rebirthing.	Monoclinic	6–7	6th	USA, South Africa
Zoisite (Hydrous calcium aluminium & silica)	Brown-reddish	Helps recovery from an illness. Is a transformation stone that turns negative into positive.	Orthorhombic	6–6.5	All	Various

Healing with Crystals

A crystal healer uses crystals as a vibrational healing tool. Clear quartz crystals are said to be the most powerful crystals. Clear quartz is a versatile stone that is useful for programming, healing and aligning all the chakras. There are also many other crystals that have unique and powerful qualities as well.

Crystal Healing is when crystals are used to help activate a person's healing energy. Crystals also create relaxation and balance for the body and soul. The crystals can be placed directly on a person's body or can be placed nearby such as on the floor. The crystals can be placed around the body intuitively or, on a specific chakra or meridian point depending on what the aim of the healing is for.

Many people wear crystals as jewellery to help protect and heal them as well. Crystals affect our electromagnetic-energy field or aura. **Crystals** allow the body to find it's natural rhythm and flow. You may use a yellow citrine to energise, a rose quartz to heal the heart or an amethyst to calm and help sleep.

Using crystals with crystal points, that point away from the body, take energy out of body while points facing towards the body help to bring energy into the space and activate what is required for healing. Sometimes I put several crystals on a client's abdomen or, near their knees when they are lying on a massage table. Sometimes I may use tape to keep crystals secure on a person's body to prevent the crystals from rolling onto the floor! If there is a physical health issue then there is an emotional root cause that needs to be addressed. Ask the crystals to help the healing process.

Some people put crystals into various shapes. These shapes may be a cross, a figure 8 pattern or a circle/oval shape. The shapes can be designed on or around a person's body.

Crystals can be placed on our hands or on our bodies to allow higher energies to move through them and into our own space. Crystal healing can be used on animals, plants or spaces.

If you are unable to get permission to do a healing then request that the energy goes to the person in mind or, to wherever it is needed in case the person's spirit does not want to receive it. Free will is important. I have used crystals on my cat and she has healed well. The crystals used to roll off her body so I would place them around her when she was still and resting. I have also imagined crystals and colours around people and pets. This is great to do if you are not near any crystals. The healing is still very effective. Our mind and intentions are very powerful! You can also place crystals on a drawing, or a photo, and leave them there for a while as they do their magic.

It is believed that warm-coloured stones – red, orange and yellow – stimulate energy flow whereas cool colours – blue, green and violet – are more calming. Tune into the vibration of each stone or crystal. Tap into its essence and commune with it. I feel that crystals also have intuitive healing powers and they know what to work on in a person's body. Also each crystal has its own crystal deva or spirit that will help direct and utilise the crystals energy for the Highest Good of all involved. Sometimes a client will choose their own crystal that I will use in the healing session or, I will intuitively pick crystals for them.

Programming

Crystals have the power to hold energies because of their clever internal structure. Programming a crystal is when you share your feelings, intentions, aims and goals with it. Focus on your heart's desire as this will help you programme the crystal. By focusing on your heart's wish allow the energy and vibration of the crystal to attract and magnetise these wishes to you. Remember what comes to you will be perfect for your Soul's learning and development.

Programme the crystal by holding it in your hand. Focus and visualise your goal and imagine the crystal is happy to receive your dreams and wishes. You can ask the crystal if it has any messages or insights for you in the way of images, colours, words or feelings.

Crystal Gazing and/or Scrying

I enjoy scrying with crystal balls. I see images as I tap into the energetic vibration of the crystal. Take your time and keep practising as these skills will grow over time. Take deep breaths to slow down your mind. Ten deep breaths will put you into a light trance. As you relax tune into the crystal and allow it to reveal its knowledge to you.

Crystal Massage

Some people use crystals for massaging. Crystals can help to relieve tension in the body, mind and soul and help to rebalance the chakras. Grab a polished stone and rub your feet or hand. How does it feel? Be creative and see how you can use the crystals energy to soothe your skin and revitalise your spirit.

Exercise: Attuning to your Crystal.

One of the best ways to get to know your crystal is to meditate with it.

1. Find a quiet comfortable spot somewhere and sit down and relax with your crystal. Take a few deep breaths.

2. Breathe in and visualise golden white light entering your body, refreshing and recharging you. Hold each breath for a moment and experience the fullness of your being. Breathe out and release any tightness or frustrations you may have.

3. Hold the crystal in your hand and hold it close to your heart. Allow you heart to receive the Divine energies of the crystal.

4. Communicate with the crystal, tell it how you are feeling and what you need right now.

5. How do you feel now after communing with your crystal?

At the end of the meditation thank the crystal and ask it to watch over you and to send you messages in the next few days via dreams, a song or some insight you may have.

Wearing Crystals

You might like to wear your crystals for support and to balance your energy.

A simple way to achieve this is to place a crystal into a small bag or pouch suspended around your neck. By wearing a crystal as jewellery you ensure that its energy merges with your aura, subtly balancing you physically and emotionally throughout the day.

- **Pendants** – This normally allows the crystal to be worn over the heart or thymus gland which controls the immune system and strengthens the energy field.
- **Earrings** – The crystal balances mental energy.
- **Bracelets and Rings** – When worn on the left side, they balance the energy we receive. Worn on the right side, they balance the energy we give or send.
- **Necklaces** – These are worn to enhance your ability to communicate, and help you lovingly speak your truth.

Heavenly Crystals

The amazing thing is we do not even need to have the real crystals to use. Even thinking about, or imagining crystals around us, is still powerful on our aura and our energy bodies.

Crystals allow portals of energy to flow through them. I like to use **Heavenly** crystals when I don't have any real ones around. This means they are on another dimension yet are very real and alive. It's just like calling in a spirit or Higher Energy.

These **Heavenly** crystals are really happy to help and support us. Just call in the energy of a heavenly crystal. You may even feel tingles or a shift in awareness when you call these crystals in. Play with them and tune into the crystal energies. This is great to do when travelling or out shopping. You may not have real crystals on you but with **Heavenly** crystals you can use them at any time!

Crystal Cave

Imagine you're in a huge Celestial Crystal Cave. Put yourself in the middle of the crystal cave and feel safe, loved and secure. Great to do at bedtime or when in need of healing. Pray and ask for what you need and visualise your goals and wishes happening for you in positive and purposeful ways.

Heavenly Crystal Healing

Heavenly Healing is when you use your intention and visions to heal. For example you can heal your health by asking the energy of a crystal to help you.

Imagine in your mind's eye this is happening as we know that the subconscious is very visual and, it doesn't know what's real or imagined. When you are having a drink of water request that the energy of a certain crystal is in the water. See it, believe it and notice what happens. No crystals were placed in the water on a physical level but, they are definitely there on a spiritual and energetic plane.

You activated the crystal healing power with the power of your mind and intentions!

Crystal Green Healing

One day I was doing a reading on a client when I saw a glowing green energy appear over the client's right shoulder. It looked like a huge green shimmering crystal. I realised the spirit world was sending healing energy to the client.

I told the client about my vision.

"My shoulder has been aching for days,"she said. "I'm glad it's receiving some healing as it needs it!"

Sometimes the spirit world will bring in healing crystalline energy to help clients heal. Other times the guides will show me, clairvoyantly, a crystal necklace, indicating that they are assisting in healing the client on some level.

Crystals – Using Pendulums

A pendulum can give you insight into how the chakras are going. The pendulum taps into the electromagnetic energy of the chakras.

It is said the inner wheel of a chakra nearly always spins clockwise yet, pendulums usually test the outside wheel of a chakra. This outer wheel holds vibration around our issues, programmed beliefs as well as our triumphs. Pendulums took me a while to get comfortable with. I now enjoy using them with clients. You will need to use a necklace, a crystal pendulum or some object that will be on a chain or string.

Bella's Chakras

The chakras are dynamic and constantly change depending on our exercise, food, sleep and thoughts. I love when I see a chakra has rebalanced itself after getting Reiki or crystal healing.

I use a pendulum to see the changes in the chakras and how the chakra has repaired and rebalanced itself. Sometimes it may reset itself immediately or it may take several sessions for the chakras to adequately rebalance.

Bella returned for her monthly session and I used the pendulum over her chakras as she lay on the massage table. They were spinning well and she reminded me how they used to be all over the place. Bella said that her Reiki sessions, along with her lifestyle changes, were helping her mentally, physically, emotionally and spiritually. It was great to see her active again and reducing her sugar and alcohol intake.

Bella was handling work better and was looking forward to taking on new adventures in her life. Her doctor said she no longer needed medication for her thyroid imbalance (5th chakra) and that he was happy with her recent blood test results.

Using a Pendulum

Hold a pendulum about 15–20cm above the chakra area. The person can lie down or you can do while sitting.

Pendulum Swings Indicate[33]:

Clockwise swing = chakra is operating well
Anticlockwise swing = chakra is processing or releasing energy
Small, tight swing = chakra may not be open enough
Large, wide swing = chakra may be too open
Vertical swing = person needs practical & logical insight in this chakra
Horizontal swing= person needs spiritual insight in this chakra
Diagonal swing = chakra needs energy and balance
No movement = Blocked energy or person not trusting the process

---

33 Dale, C. (2013) *The Subtle Body Practsie manual*, p.322, Sounds True, US.

Note: Crystal pendulums can heal the chakras so after using them, re-test the chakras and you may find they have rebalanced themselves.

Notice what chakras have the same spin. Sometimes the heart and 3rd eye chakras spins are similar as these chakras are energetically connected. Look at what chakras may be compensating or counter-balancing for another chakra. Is one chakra overworking because another chakra is weak?

You can focus on the imbalanced chakra and use the pendulum to answer yes or no questions to tell you approximately what age the block began or what the issue is about. To work out what is a "yes" or "no" response with the chakra, ask it to show you. You may prefer to ask your intuition for insights and open up your clairs to receive insight about the chakras.

Glow on Palms:

I remember teaching a palmistry course one weekend. I asked Amy to come out the front for a palm reading so I could do a demonstration for the students. Amy placed her palm, facing up, on a small cushion. I was surprised to see energy bouncing up off her hand.

Clairvoyantly I could see soft hues of colours vibrate from her palms. I told the group what I saw. We had just done a crystal meditation and each student had held a quartz in their palms while they meditated.

This really shows the amazing power of crystals and the effects they have on our energy and vibration.

"When we begin to take ownership of the so-called unlovable parts of ourselves, compassion is born, making it easier to love and accept ourselves. It also becomes much easier to accept and love others for who they are, instead of projecting our disowned lost soul pieces onto them."[34]

Crystal Ray Healing

I had a student in my Crystal Ray healing course who was a popular massage therapist in Canberra. He sent me an email a few weeks after the course saying how he found the techniques he learnt in the course to be very powerful with his clients. He also said the results were amazing and he thanked me profusely for the opportunity to do the course.

---

34 Wolf, L. (2009) *Shamanic Breathwork* (p.138) Bear & Company, Vermont.

I have developed a Crystal Ray Healing protocol for you to use in your healing sessions.

* CRYSTAL RAY HEALING PROTOCOL *

① **Prepare room/space:** you may need pillows, sheets, blanket, music, crystals, candles, water.

② **Connect with client.** Smile and ask them how their day has been. Find out why they are seeking a healing. Ask them to tell you 3 feelings or emotions they have right now that they would like to heal.

③ **Explain** to the client about the session and get their permission to use crystals/touch, etc. Ask client to lay face down (or up) on the massage table. You could also use a chair or couch.

④ **Open your third eye** and have a look at the clients aura, energy and chakras. Call in Guides & and Higher Energies, who love you unconditionally, to support you both. Imagine the room is filled with Gold/White Light Energy. Offer a prayer, or intention to the universe, about the aim of this healing session. Place crystals (that you choose or they have chosen) in areas such as on the floor or on their body.

⑤ **Ask client to breathe** (you also!) in deeply beautiful coloured energy. Press along their body gently to relax them using gentle hand pressure. Do a figure 8 pattern over their back. Place your hands on the back of their knees. Now hold their ankles gently. Move up to their head and place one hand behind their heart area and another hand on the back of their head. Touch person appropriately and with respect.

⑥ **Visualisation** Turn client over onto their back, if necessary. Ask the person to continue relaxing deep breaths and as they do suggest that they are going into a deeply relaxed state every time they breathe in and out. Ask them to imagine that they are going to the most serene natural place and for them to feel their feet firmly planted on the ground, to hear the sounds, feel the gentle breeze, look at the beautiful landscapes around them. Ask them, to walk to a gorgeous crystal garden with flowers, harps playing and their Higher Self/Guide is there. In the Crystal garden, they see a comfortable lounge and they lay on it, feet up and head back, feeling 10 times more deeply relaxed as they do this.

⑦ **Optional:** You say that you're going to ask their subconscious about the feelings and words they told you earlier in step 2. For example: they felt anger, disappointment, sadness. Ask that deeper part of them to tell you an age or a time that those feelings happened to them. e.g. "Breathe deeply and relax. Take yourself back to a time where you felt anger, disappointment sadness." You ask them to share with you what they see (they may see a movie, a colour, a scene, an image, a person or an age).

E.g. if they said aged 6 you get them to imagine the 6yr-old sitting beside them on the lounge holding their hand in the crystal garden. You ask them to tune into that younger part of them and sense what the child feels, thinks, looks like and share these insights. The younger self lies down on the lounge with them. They hug. You describe how relaxed, bonded and united they both are and how healing has occurred. Talk to the younger self. Send golden, white light healing energy to the memories they shared.

⑧ **Ask again** "Breathe deeply and relax. Take yourself back to another time where you felt anger, disappointment, sadness." Then ask them to share with you what they see (they may see a movie, a colour, a scene, an image, a person or an age).

The **crystals** you have used on the person will also attract and channel energy to the parts of the body that person most needs it. (You also will get a healing as the energy will also be cleansing and healing your aura too.)

⑨ You may wish to **touch client's** feet before you help them up off the table. Offer them a drink of water. Ask the client how they're feeling and chat about any experiences you both may have had during the Crystal Ray Healing session. Tell the client to keep hydrated in the next few days and if

229

they get loose bowels it just means emotional energy and clearing is been released through their body/chakras. Ask them to be gentle on themselves over the next few days and that any crying is a good release of pent-up emotions. They can journal their emotions also if they wish. Refer clients to other modalities if you feel they may need extra support.

⑩ **Your Self-care:** Close your eyes, place your palms towards the floor, and as you breathe out allow any excess energy to go down to the earth to be transformed into light. Have an aromatherapy bath. Add in essential oils, a herbal teabag (like camomile) or Epsom salts (1/2 cup) or sea salts (1/2 cup). A bath is also a brilliant way to cleanse and relax your nervous system.

Anna's CRYSTAL GEM ELIXIR (Indirect Method)

Direct method is where crystals go directly into water. Some people do this if it's safe but as a Naturopath I feel it's safer to do indirect method as some crystals leach out or break down in the water so I personally feel it's best to be careful. Crystals ending in "ite" usually dissolve in water!

Place a small glass bowl of crystals inside a bigger glass bowl. Put water in bigger glass bowl only. You can use spring, distilled or, cooled down boiled water. Leave the two glass bowls outside for a few hours in the sunlight or moonlight.

Choose a few crystals to go into the smaller bowl only so they are not in direct contact with the water in the bigger bowl. Choose crystals that you feel drawn to.

The Crystals I used were:

Pyrite Chakra: Solar plexus. Abundance, wealth. Heals viruses.

Jade Chakra: Base & heart. Reproductive health + youthfulness.

Sodalite Chakra: Brow & throat. Travel, writing, BP, menopause.

Hematite Chakra: Base. Energy, cycles. Name in Greek means blood. Do not wear if you or your client have a pacemaker. Called Lawyers stone as helps in court cases.

Amazonite Chakra: Heart & Throat. Stone of Courage, Truth and Prosperity. Helps communication and balances the feminine and masculine within us.

Labradorite Chakra: Brow & base. Stone of magic. Shaman crystal. past lives and Akashic records. Also for fun and adventure!

Moonstone Chakra: Sacral. Hormones and allergies. Hopes and goal setting.

Fluorite Chakra: Brow & heart. Helps with electromagnetic stress from phones and computers.

Rose Quartz Chakra: Heart. Helps Depression, forgiveness, self-love and sleep patterns.

Smoky Quartz Chakra: Base. Helps anxiety, insomnia, psychic attack, pain, panic attacks & sadness. Stone of power. Brings strength and stability.

The energy of the crystals has now permeated energetically into the water in the bigger bowl. You can use the elixir in sprays, in the bath, or as a scent. You can put it in an oil diffuser. You can also add this divine elixir to an oil like macadamia and use it as a body cream.

Be creative! I have a bottle of my elixir in my office and clinic. I have also used it on clients and it activated their chakras with fascinating results.

Elixir Recipe

Use 1 ¼ cup Elixir + 1/3 cup apple cider vinegar. This will last 1 year if taking it internally. If using it externally can last up to 3 years.

Exercise: White Hall

1. Imagine you are in a white hall. The walls are white, the floor is white and the roof is white. The energy in the room is powerful yet tranquil, loving and gentle.

2. Imagine looking at yourself, sitting in the white hall. Ask to be shown what's in the white hall around you. (Hold a crystal in your hand or just set your intention to see from your 3rd eye.)

3. Close your eyes if you wish or, leave them open.

4. Open your 3rd eye vision to 'see' the images, shapes, colours and vibrations that appear around you.

5. Ask for more clarity if you need the images to be clearer.

6. Imagine someone else sitting in the white hall and ask to be shown images, guides, totem animals or loved ones around them.

7. Be creative and explore this all knowing, all wise great white hall.

8. You may be surprised at what you see!

Interesting Crystal Facts

In the Earth's crust, the most abundant minerals are Feldspars (about 40–60%) and Quartz (about 30–50%). Quartz makes up 20% of granite rocks found on the continental plates and Feldspar makes up 65%.

Basalt is the rock underlying the ocean basins. It is composed of 20% Quartz and 65% Feldspar as well.[35]

I was keen to find more about this abundant mineral feldspar and the encyclopedia stated: "The term feldspar actually covers a whole family of minerals, all of which consist of a framework of aluminum, oxygen, and silicon atoms plus an additive, usually potassium, sodium, or calcium."[36]

---

35 www.quora.com/geology
36 www.encyclopedia.com/earth

Amethyst Fact: Some amethysts have triangles on their points. These are called Trigonic Amethysts. It is believed that Trigonics are a "race of star beings who wish to assist the consciousness-shift of planet Earth and to bring peace to all."[37]

What is the Earth made up of?

When we connect to the crystals and minerals in the earth, we can tap into their energy. Here's a peek into what lies beneath us!

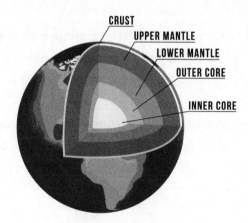

Figure 15.2

Oceans cover 70% of the Earth's surface.

There are 3 main layers to the earth:

Earth's crust is between 0 and 75 km deep. This crust is made up of 47% oxygen, 27% Silicon, 8% aluminium and smaller amounts of iron (5%), calcium (4%), magnesium (4%). Crust also has 2% sodium and potassium.[38]

The Earth's mantle makes up 67% of our Earth. "It is composed mostly of silicate rocks rich in magnesium and iron."[39] Crystals are found in our earth. Rocks that are found inside the Earth's mantle

---

37 Hall, J. (2013) *Encylopedia of crystals*, Octopus, London.
38 www.space.com/1777
39 www.space.com/1777

are: olivine, pyroxenes, spinel, and garnet.[40] *Note: Olivine is also called peridot and chrysolite.*

Earth's Core: The earth's core is about the size of the moon.[41] This centre core is made of iron. What's strange is that this iron inner core spins at a different speed to the rest of the earth! This is said to affect the Earth's magnetic field. This centre iron core is also enclosed by a liquid made of nickel and iron.[42]

Sacred Geometry

Platonic solids are made up of the 5 shapes that make up our universe. The five platonic solids are: hexahedron (cube), octahedron (double inverted pyramid), tetrahedron (pyramid), icosohedron and dodecahedron.

The first four shapes link with the elements: earth (hexahedron), air (octahedron), fire (tetrahedron) and water (icosohedron), with the fifth, dodecahedron, representing heaven, sky or the Universe.

Table 15.4

Polyhedron	Vertices (Apex)	Faces	Element
hexahedron	8	6	Earth
octahedron	6	8	Air
tetrahedron	4	4	Fire
icosahedron	12	20	Water
dodecahedron	20	12	Universe

---

40 www.universetoday.com
41 www.live.science.com
42 www.space.com

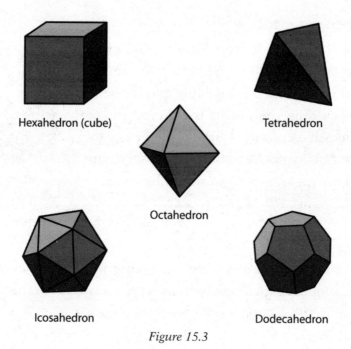

Hexahedron (cube)

Tetrahedron

Octahedron

Icosahedron

Dodecahedron

Figure 15.3

Metatron's Cube

Metatron's cube is a very powerful symbol as it contains the 5 platonic solids which are said to make up the universe.

Merkaba

Figure 15.4

The Merkaba is made of two tetrahedron (pyramids) in opposite directions. By imagining, wearing or holding a merkaba you can open up higher chakras as it's said to activate the pineal gland in the brain. Tetrahedrons are linked to the element of fire so I feel it activates the kundalini which allows the higher chakras to expand and open. The merkaba is a protective shape!

Figure 15.5

Flower of Life

Flower of Life is a flower pattern containing many overlapping circles. The Flower of Life is a wonderful pattern used for healing and for being a window to other realms. It is believed to contain the Akashic records. I have a picture of the Flower of Life symbol at home that I scry with. I like to blur my eyes and go into a light trance state as the image reveals its messages to me.

Figure 15.6

Fibonacci

The Fibonacci sequence is a number pattern. The numbers in the Fibonacci sequence total the 2 previous numbers (except the very first 2 numbers in the sequence). The sequence goes 0, 1, 1, 2, 3, 5, 8, 13, 21, 34 and so on.

Fibonacci numbers are found in nature from sunflowers to galaxies. Sunflowers seeds, pinecones, pineapples and, some seashells and flowers are arranged in a Fibonacci spiral pattern.[43] It is said that any two sequential Fibonacci numbers have a ratio very close to the Golden Ratio which is about 1.618. The larger the pair of Fibonacci numbers, the closer it is to the Golden ratio and golden spiral.[44]

Golden Ratio

The Golden ratio pattern (see picture) can be found in nature and science[45].

Flower petals: The number of petals on some flowers resemble the Fibonacci sequence.

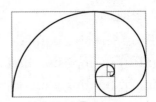

Figure 15.7

---

43 http://mathforum.org/library/drmath/view/52679.html
44 http://www.goldennumber.net/spirals/
45 http://www.livescience.com/37704-phi-golden-ratio.html

Pinecones: The spiral pattern of the seed pods spiral upward in opposite directions. The spirals seems to match Fibonacci numbers.
Tree branches: Some tree branches grow in a Fibonacci sequence.
Shells: Many shells have patterns similar to the Golden spiral.
Spiral galaxies: The shape of the spiral is like the Golden spiral.
Hurricanes: Hurricanes also resemble the Golden spiral.

Geometric Patterns

Many things around us are designed in unique geometric patterns from the shape of our DNA, our cornea, diamonds, crystals and stars.

Sacred Geometry Exercise:

1. Have an intention of what you need right now so the symbols can assist you and align with your consciousness and energies.

2. Ask to be shown which symbol you need right now.

3. Imagine yourself surrounded by this sacred shape. Allow it to come into your mind or, focus on the shape if you have a picture or image of it nearby.

Allow yourself to merge with the symbol's energy and healing power. Trust that what you need will come to you.

CHAPTER 16

Your Wellbeing &
Achieving your Goals

"The best job of all is doing something that doesn't feel like a job at all."[46]

It's great to have goals but oftentimes we have to work out how to stop blocking our success.

Here are some hints and tips to help you embrace your potential and increase your vitality so you can achieve your goals.

Move Your Body

Our bodies are designed to move. When we exercise we move our chakras, our glands and our organs. Exercise helps shift stuck energy that's blocked in our body from food and emotions. Your soul is happier being connected to your body if you exercise and are well nourished.

---

46 Hendricks, G. (2009) *The Big Leap* (p.213), Harper Collins, NY.

Relaxing and stretching is also important. Doing 10–20 minute meditation and yoga sessions can help you relax and allows you to better tune into the psychic realms.

Of course there are always reasons why we can't exercise, "It's too hot, too cold, not enough time…" the weather will always be variable outdoors. We can make excuses or we can just do it. What you decide is what you create. How do you want to live? How do you want to feel? You are the Master of you own destiny. Create a life that brings you good energy, fun and a smile on your face.

I use crystals, Reiki or self-hypnosis to help me if I feel I need some healing. Sometimes my soul wants to have a bath, cry, read, do tarot, walk or chat. We are lucky we have choices to whatever method resonates with us. I also like to ask my Guide for help. As humans we are meant to be Perfectly Imperfect. I love this wise quote from a picture in my home:

"Our greatest glory is not in never falling, but in rising every time we fall."

I remember one day feeling flat and wondering why I was not focusing on my projects. I laid down and did a visualisation/self-hypnosis and I took myself into a beautiful garden. There I met a part of me that was struggling. I held her hand and asked her telepathically (from my mind to her mind) what was going on & how she felt. She told me about her fears and her feelings. I asked her what she needed from me to feel happier.

She was a part of my inner self and when my inner self is happy then my outer world will reflect this. This whole process only took a few minutes of time. I then finished off this mini-visualisation by seeing myself achieving my goals in the future. I did this several times over the next week and this helped me get back on track. This simple exercise is effective, easy and powerful.

Exercise: Connection Visualisation

1. Breathe deeply, relax and imagine a beautiful garden.
2. Call forth a part of you that is tense or not at ease.
3. Connect with and send love to this part of you.
4. Ask that part of you what was going on & how it feels. What does that part of you need right now?
5. See yourself achieving your goals in the future.

Repeat when necessary so it embeds deeply into your subconscious.

Be creative and add extra steps to this visualisation. You'll be surprised what your subconscious and superconscious want to share with you.

You are here for a reason. You are LOVE and you need to dance the love dance every day. Make yourself and others smile as humour is such lovely light energy! Go within and connect often and "see", hear or feel what is around you.

Let the Universe bond with you as it's massive and SO wants to help you – just ASK. Call the stars in, the planets, the Higher Energies to make this earth plane the best it can be for you.

Be the Best Human Warrior out here. Best of all Love yourself enough to strive forward with dignity, presence and power.

Eva's Plan

Eva, a relative of mine, complained to me that she can never get her goals achieved. She acknowledges that she spends a lot of time on social media and watching television shows. Eva asked me for help so we did a visualisation and healing together.

We also worked out a plan so she could do simple things each day that worked towards achieving her goals. She still had time to socialise but Eva realised she had been wasting lots of time doing mindless activities.

Eva became more focused and felt proud that she was finally moving forward in life.

Tips for Success

- Limit social media. Time to put the pet in its cage – so to speak!

- Set aside blocks of time to focus. Make time to expand, grow and achieve.

- Cut back on social events. Say yes to some events and no to others so you have more time for your projects.

- Remove tempting phones and technology from your workspace. I put my mobile phone into another room. I can hear the phone if it rings but it's not within arms reach so I can't fiddle with it. Clean up later. You may need to do your projects with a messy house some days. It's easy to divert your attention and do other jobs, but they can always wait.

- Stock up your fridge with healthy foods and snacks to keep your brain balanced and healthy.

- Tell your family that you have set goals and give them extra hugs!

What happens when you start to get successful? Your inner self may pull you down to a comfy level for fear that doing well may cause too many changes in your life.

Reassure your fears that your success will help others and that you deserve to progress and achieve in life as it's healthy, natural and normal. Allow success to be a healthy by-product of your commitment, focus, happiness and vitality.

A Gift you can give yourself is to plan. The old saying "if we fail to plan, we plan to fail" is so true.

Exercise: Your Dreams and Visions

Write down answers to these questions, as writing allows you to hear your inner voice.

1. My purpose in life is to …
2. My heart desires are …
3. I deserve to...
4. My goals are …
5. I need …
6. I can help myself by…
7. My fears are …
8. I can comfort myself by …
9. I enjoy …
10. I am good at …
11. I can offer this planet …
12. My life's purpose in this lifetime is …

Your Progress

We can block our progress by keeping ourselves small. Instead of standing up tall and allowing the flow of life to guide us, we stay small and feel like the ceiling is crushing down on us.

The real ceiling is higher, we have just created a false ceiling that is keeping us down. This false ceiling is made up of untrue beliefs and ideas such as – "I'm not good enough; Others are better than me; Success means others will be threatened by me." Or thinking "I do not have what it takes to be successful; I'm lazy; I'm slack like my… ; I never do anything right."

These false thoughts appear in your life and show up as worry, blame, sickness, hurt, fighting/arguing; not listening to your feelings, getting lost, not keeping agreements/appointments, not communicating well to others, not accepting compliments.[47]

Maybe your self-talk says "going to the next level means people may look at me differently and not understand me."

Do you get more of a buzz from whinging and staying at the same level you've been in for years or, are you happy to outgrow where you are now and move into a new space, a new life?

Other signs of blocking our soul's path is dating the wrong people, getting caught up in other people's drama; being a drama queen/king; seeing faults easily; wasting time, getting bored, feeling a victim and, that everyone else is the problem, feeling defeated, using self-defeating strategies such as over-eating/spending/gambling/drinking/smoking, etc.

Life can be an up and down journey. The people who are successful are the ones who learn from their experiences. They learn new strategies and ways of responding to life's challenges. Thinking outside the box, gaining knowledge and, being honest and respectful, helps us stay in our heart and ride the waves of this lifetime.

Some people say they want to change but they do not put action behind the words. Other people are motivated to walk their talk. It's great to see people create meaningful and profound changes in their lives. It's easier than you think. It all starts with one small step…

Abundance is Coming

Author Louise Hay used to say that when we are focused on our passions the money will follow. When our heart and spirit are in alignment and, we know love, truth and peace, then money will find us.

When a client sends me a message about how their healing has progressed well, I get tears in my eyes. I am still in awe of the profound healing capacity of the Human Spirit. Through creativity, faith,

---

47 Hendricks, G. (2009) *The Big leap* (p.111), Harper Collins, NY.

passion and determination we can make a difference in our lives, and others. Know that you are profoundly guided and protected and that you will never be given more than you can handle.

"Money is simply spiritual energy in motion."[48]

Criticism and Blame

How often do you criticise yourself and others? Criticism and blame are said to be addictions. Is the monkey mind chattering and repeating bad thoughts over and over in your mind? Time to put the monkey in a cage. Let the positive thoughts flow through your mind.

Replenish and fertilise new ideas while creating a garden with positive words and thoughts. Negativity can block the flow of energy. How often you are putting down yourself or others? Each time a negative thought runs through your head like "I'm stupid" or "I never do anything well" change it to "I'm doing my best. I am on this earth to learn. It's OK to make mistakes", "I will do better next time." "I am in charge of my life", "I am loved", "I see good things happening for me in life."

"Criticism and blaming are like being in a hypnotic trance."[49]

The Mother Teresa Effect

It seems that watching someone do kinds things keeps you healthy and happier. Dr Hamilton[50] states that when we help others the hormone, oxytocin is made. Oxytocin is good for our heart. Some people say there's a "helper's high" feeling from being of service. Being kind

---

48 Hendricks, G. (2009) *The Big Leap* (p.203), Harper Collins, NY.
49 Hendricks, G. (2009) *The Big Leap*, Harper Collins, NY.
50 http://drdavidhamilton.com/

can help the immune system. A study[51] from Harvard University, showed students a 50 minute Mother Teresa video where she was doing kind acts.

The students who watched the Mother Teresa video benefitted in positive ways as their saliva tests showed an increase in IgA levels- which meant their immune system had improved.

Do kind actions for your health or even just imagine kind acts and you'll still receive the benefits!

Food

Being a naturopath and nutritionist I had to include food in this book! What we put into our mouths is so important to our overall health.

We have a huge amount of obesity in the world. Also there has been an increase in mental-health issues over the last 20 years.

This book is about psychic, healing and the cosmos and, if we are energy, then the food we eat is energy too. Food is a vibration just like we are. Our relationship to food changes as we walk along our earth path. When we befriend food we can befriend our soul; as food is the fuel for our mind, body and soul. When we feed ourselves nutritious food our intuition grows. If our body feels strong then our soul is aligned with our purpose.

A 2016 health report on Canberra, in Australia (our capital city) states that 63% of adults are now overweight or obese. A shocking statistic! There is also an increase in anxiety levels. If you smoke and/ or do not exercise you are more at risk of being depressed.

Dementia is rising rapidly due to our high sugar intake, poor sleep and lack of movement. You are more likely to have mental-health issues if you are overweight or obese; are inactive, smoke or use alcohol.

---

51 https://lifelabs.psychologies.co.uk/users/1025-dr-david-r-hamilton/posts/874-the-mother-theresa-effect

Table 16.1

1995 in Australia, Canberra	2014 in Australia, Canberra
21% Smoke	10% Smoke
40% Adults overweight or obese	63% Adults overweight or obese
25% Cancer top a cause of death 24% Men; 15% women: Heart disease	29% Cancer top a cause of death 28% Heart disease
3% Adults report having emotional issues/tension	17% Adults having diagnosis mental disorder

Craving for certain foods can mean emotions (energy in motion) need to be dealt with. Sometimes I keep eating. I keep returning to the pantry cupboard to hunt for more food. My hunger does not seem to be filled up no matter what I eat. I then realise it may be an emotional issue that I'm feeding.

I need to do something to rebalance my energies and feel my emotions. I may imagine a waterfall cleansing my aura. I may hold a crystal, do hands-on healing or go for a walk. This will relax my nervous system and the wanting to overeat subsides.

The foods we reach for tell us about our feelings and what our physical body may or may not need. Food directly affects our chakras, hormones, energy levels and intuition. Making good food choices is important for you.

I know when I eat good clean food I feel emotionally better. When I eat organic foods my behaviour is happier and I feel more content. Organic food has less herbicides and pesticides on them. The quality of organic food is superior and although it is often more expensive it is worth it as your body will greatly benefit.

If you are eating a piece of birthday cake and your internal self-talk is saying "oh, I shouldn't be eating this, it's going to make me fat..." then, your cells will hear your thoughts and this will affect the way you digest the food.

Instead you may choose to say internally "I'm enjoying this cake, it's a pleasure to eat it. Thank you food. I am enjoying your flavours." Food is a gift from our planet to help put nutrients into our bodies and to help us thrive and live. Enjoy the occasional treat and strive for balance in your diet rather than berate yourself for anything you may be eating.

However try to avoid low quality foods, particularly any with preservatives and additives in them as they do not resonate well with the chakras in your body. The less junk food you have at home the less likely you will be tempted to ravish them.

Hydrating your body with water, herbal teas, fruit and vegetables will help your cells function better for you.

Getting 7–8 hours of sleep, at least five nights a week, is really beneficial for your mind and body.

Your Reflections

The way your parents treated food may affect the way you do too. How did your parents engage with food/s and drinks?

Was it a friend or the enemy? Was it constantly affecting the way they behaved? Was it a love/hate relationship or did they honour the energy of food?

You may also like to reflect on these questions. Write down your answers if you wish.

1. Before I eat I feel...

2. When I eat I feel...

3. After I eat I feel...

4. I crave...

Food diaries are useful to help you see the patterns you have around food. People who are stressed are using up a lot of minerals in their body so they will crave sugar and junk foods, which contain no nutrition for your body! Research[52] now shows that junk food negatively affects our emotions, learning and memory. It is said we binge on food we are allergic too. It's good to have healthy snacks nearby so you can refuel your body in healthy ways.

Once you have a good relationship with food then you can spend your energy on other things that matter in life. Our relationship with food is an ongoing one just like our human relationships. Sometimes we need to learn about what makes for a happy food relationship!

This **Food Cravings** grid highlights some of the emotions linked to the foods we eat.

Table 16.2

FOOD CRAVINGS	Emotions linked to these foods:
Wheat (e.g. pasta, bread)	Lonely, frustrated, bored, no purpose in life (Find your inner joy in life)
Salty (e.g. chips, crackers, seasonings)	Stressed, uptight (Need to relax and breathe deeply)
Sugar (e.g. lollies, cakes, alcohol, ice-cream, chocolate)	Depressed, worried (May be lacking minerals such as magnesium)
Crunchy (e.g. biscuits, chips)	Angry, tense (Learn good communication skills, open your heart)
Cheese and Dairy products	Denying your feelings & inner voice (Listen to your heart's wishes, do gentle exercise)
Soft foods (e.g. cream)	Anxious (Soothe self by having massages, baths, walks, fun)

---

52 http://www.deakin.edu.au/about-deakin/media-releases/articles/does-junk-food-shrink-your-brain

Creating Positive Energy

Soothing music has been shown to relax us and reduce cortisol. Music also helps us focus on tasks. I find I work more efficiently if I have soft, calming music playing in the background.

Research shows that people in a good mood will eat better foods and make better food choices.

People in a negative mood will make more poor food choices. Lifting our mood and focusing attention on positive actions will affect the way we eat and the way we do activities.

Healing Josey

Josey was a single 44-year-old accountant. She desired a loving partner but didn't feel ready for dating. "I need to focus on being a good friend to myself first," she told me.

Josey noticed that the time between when she came home from work and when she went to bed was "dangerous." She said she drank and ate too much food in this "dangerous" time as she felt lonely, frustrated and bored with life. Her body was riddled with arthritis and her hair was thinning.

We spent several sessions looking at her nutrition and unresolved emotions. We did Reiki, shamanic and crystal healing to help her healing. One day Josie joyfully marched into my office saying how her health had dramatically improved. Her face glowed and she had lost weight.

Josie's whole outlook on life had shifted. The skeletons from the past were no longer living in her head and she was enjoying walking, doing yoga and eating better. Josie dramatically cut down on sugar, wheat and alcohol and couldn't believe the difference in how it helped her sleep, relax and be happier. People at work were commenting on the noticeable changes.

Josie's hair began to grow back and she was able to move better as her arthritis was healing.

The Power of Oils

Essential oils are energy and they have a place in your psychic and healing endeavours. Everything is energy and by tapping into the benefits of oils we can further help our mind, body and soul. The more our aura and energy field is in harmony the better we will be in all areas of our lives. To be a clear channel for energy it's vital to live a life where you use products that enhance your mood and wellbeing.

"Harmful chemicals can get into your body if you breathe, eat, or drink them or if they are absorbed through your skin."[53]

In my 20s I decided to adopt a cleaner lifestyle to help my overall health. One of the best things I ever did was adopt healthy ways to clean my home. This reduced the amount of chemicals I would breathe into my body. Also my skin absorbed less chemicals from my homemade creams and cleaning products. Now research is showing that harsh chemicals are imbalancing our hormones (chakras) and are causing health problems.[54]

---

53 https://www.atsdr.cdc.gov/emes/public/docs/health%20effects%20of%20chemical%20
   exposure%20fs.pdf
54 https://www.atsdr.cdc.gov/emes/public/docs/health%20effects%20of%20chemical%20
   exposure%20fs.pdf

Essential Oils are fabulous to use in homemade products to replace chemicals and artificial perfumes. Organic essential oils are wonderful to use as they are purer.

Here are some simple ideas for you that are very effective and smell great! Your skin, hormones and body will find these products harmonious for your body, mind and soul.[55] Research shows oils connect with the amygdala, in our brain, which positively affects our emotions and wellbeing. Oils on the skin are effective and can help our behaviour and immune system. I regularly use oils in my home and office and I find them very effective.

Essential Oils

Here's a list of some useful essential oils.

Bergamot: a citrus-type oil that helps the skin to heal.

Camomile: very good for the treatment of nervous conditions and insomnia. It is antibacterial and antiseptic but is mostly valued for its anti-inflammatory properties.

Citronella: a repellent that works well with eucalyptus and lemon to keep the mosquitoes & insects away.

Eucalyptus: helps with inflammation and the immune system.

Frankincense: has a calming effect on emotions. Frankincense can also help lessen wrinkles in the skin. Add it to coconut oil and use as a skin cream.

Geranium: is used in skin care. It has antiseptic and astringent properties and has been called a natural anti-depressant.

Lavender: great for calming and relaxing. Is good for headaches, sleep, allergies, and tension. Queen of the oils!

Lemon: an antibacterial oil, good for healing and is great for cleaning & revitalising the home.

---

55 https://www.cancer.gov/about-cancer/treatment/cam/patient/aromatherapy-pdq#section/_3

Lemongrass: clears the mind and increases psychic awareness. Promotes hope and peace in oneself.

Lime oil: a very refreshing scent that is good as a disinfectant.

Neroli: eases anxiety and depression. Helps with self-confidence.

Orange: promotes calm and aids digestion.

Peppermint: helps digestion as well as clarity and alertness. Helps in keeping away mice, mosquitoes & ants.

Rose Geranium: gentle loving oil that heals the heart and grounds the spirit.

Rosemary: this is one of the most stimulating and relaxing oils. Eases arthritis and cramps. Alleviates hair loss and dandruff.

Sandalwood: can be placed on the wrists to heighten intuition; helps sleep and relaxation.

Tea Tree: antifungal, antibacterial, antiviral and has a powerful antiseptic action. Can be used in the treatment of fungal infections, candida infections, acne, etc. (Antiseptic means it prevents growth of microorganisms such as bacteria, virus, or fungus.)

Ylang-ylang: a calming oil that enhances spiritual awareness.

Some Uses of Essential Oils

Body Lotion: Mix coconut oil and essential oils for a beautiful body lotion.

Breath: Use a drop of peppermint essential oil to freshen your breath.

Clean Home: Use boiled water that has been cooled down. Put water in a spray bottle and add a few drops of oils such as tea tree, lavender and eucalyptus. Works well as a disinfectant.

Cleanser: Use boiled water that has been cooled down. Add oils to baking soda and mix into a nice consistency. Great for cleaning around the home.

Lip balm: Combine coconut oil and drops of your favourite essential oils to moisturise your lips. Shea butter can be used too as it has a creamy consistency.

Natural perfume or deodorant: Dab 1–2 drops of essential oil on your wrist or, use a spray bottle where you can dilute the essential oils with water. Much healthier to use than perfumes which may have chemicals in them.

Nice odour: Place oil into a cotton ball to help odour and purify an area. Lemon oil and tea tree are good to use.

Oils at home/work: Use an oil diffuser to cleanse the air in your home. Helps relax the energy in the house as smells affect the emotional centres in our brain.

Scrub (Face): Mix a few drops of an essential oil with organic almond oil then, add rock salt to make your own face scrub.

Scrub (Sinks and Basins): ½ cup of baking soda, ½ cup of vinegar and a few drops of bergamot or lime oil will help to clean the tubs and sinks.

Sleep: Sprinkle, or spray, a few drops of lavender on your pillow or wrist to help you go to sleep.

Stillness: Use frankincense or sandalwood essential oil while meditating to enhance spiritual awareness.

Relaxing bath: Add lavender or chamomile oils to a cup of epsom salts/sea salt then have a warm bath to cleanse and rejuvenate the body.

Wash food: To clean fruit and vegetables, add two drops of lemon oil to a large bowl of water then wash gently.

Washing machine: I like to add eucalyptus oil into my washing. I add a few drops of eucalyptus to 2 cups of cooled down boiled water. This is stored in my laundry cupboard so I can add a splash to each clothes wash.

Note: Test the skin for oil sensitivity & do not use if there is redness or itchiness. Check with your health professional before using essential oils.

> "When you feel an emotion, a pattern of brain chemistry follows it."[56]

Harmony

I believe that when your internal world becomes balanced then your outer world will reflect this. When we heal and evolve we may find ourselves keen to clean the environment around us. When we remove our emotional clutter then we will want to remove the physical clutter too.

Exercise: Wheel Breathing

Wheel Breathing is great when you want instant energy, calm and focus.

1. Breathe in to the count of 6 then out for 6 counts. For example, Breathe in and silently count 1,2,3,4,5,6 then breathe out 1,2,3,4,5,6. Do this continuously for a few moments to ground and centre you.

2. Now increase the breathing to 2 breaths in and 2 breaths out for a few moments. Feel the movement of your diaphragm and abdomen as they move up and down. Be aware of the oxygen, air and life-force that is circulating round your body, giving you energy, strength and vitality to all of your cells.

3. Finish with slowing down the breath (wheel) again. Breathe in to the count of 6 then out for 6 counts. Breathe in 1,2,3,4,5,6 then out 1,2,3,4,5,6. Do this continuously for a few moments to relax you.

---

56 http://drdavidhamilton.com/the-4-components-of-emotion/

Optimists Vs Pessimists

Neuroscientists[57] have found that people who have a happier disposition are more optimistic and have more activity occurring on the left side of the brain (prefrontal cortex).

Optimistic people have better moods and relationships, are more successful and have better physical health. They have stronger immune systems so they tend to live longer.

Pessimistic people are "eight times more likely to be depressed than optimists."[58]

Our nervous system has 2 parts:

1. The sympathetic nervous system which is the fight, flight, freeze part. It is activated more when we feel worried or stressed.

2. The parasympathetic nervous system is where our bodies rest and relax.

The good news is that mindful breathing exercises, like meditation and yoga increase our parasympathetic nervous system so we feel more relaxed and connected to self and others.

Yoga

As a yoga teacher I'm excited to add yoga exercises to this book as yoga is a great way to tap into your parasympathetic nervous system which is your rest and digest system.

Most weeks I go outside to do 10–20 minutes of yoga and I'm amazed at the relaxation, peacefulness and stillness that comes over me after stretching, breathing and being mindful. The yoga poses below are fabulous for your hormones, energy levels and chakras.

---

57 http://reset.me/story/this-is-what-happens-to-your-brain-when-you-experience-happiness/
58 http://reset.me/story/this-is-what-happens-to-your-brain-when-you-experience-happiness/

You'll be amazed at how you feel after doing these yoga exercises and it doesn't take very long to do. **Please check with your Doctor or Health professional before doing yoga or exercise.**

Table 16.3

Yoga Poses	
1. Cat-Cow Pose *Stretches the hips, abdomen and back. Massages the organs like the kidneys and adrenal glands.* Start on all fours with hands directly under shoulders, and knees under your hips. Cow Pose: Inhale as you drop your belly towards the mat. Now lift your chin and chest, and look up. Cat Pose: As you exhale, draw your belly into your spine and round your back toward the ceiling/sky like a cat stretching its back. Inhale and repeat a few times.	**2. Downward Dog Pose** *Elongates spine and strengthens arms and legs.* Start on all fours with hands directly under shoulders, knees under your hips. Slowly move your hips up towards the ceiling/sky, bringing your body into an upside down V. Feet should be hip-width apart, knees slightly bent. Relax head and repeat slowly and mindfully. Move your knees and hips if you wish to get a gentle movement.
3. Low Lunge Pose *Good for quadriceps, hamstrings and hips.* Begin in Downward-Facing Dog. When you exhale, step your right foot forward between your hands. Lower down onto your left knee. Lower your left knee to the floor and, keeping the right knee in place, slide left back so you feel a gentle stretch in leg.	**4. Cobra Pose** *Opens the chest and strengthens the core body. Helps align the spine and is good for kidneys and your nervous system.* Lie on your belly, with the chin near the floor, palms flat on floor and near the shoulders; legs together. With the elbows close to your sides, press down into the palms and use the arms to lift you up. Relax and drop the shoulders down and back. Push the chest gently forward. Breathe and hold for a few breaths. Now exhale and slowly lower the chest and head to the floor. Turn the head to one side and rest. Repeat.

5.Child Pose	6. Bridge Pose
Calms mind and stretches the back and hips.	*Stretches chest, thighs & spine.*
Sit up comfortably on your heels. Roll your torso forward, bringing your forehead forward extending your arms in front of you. Hold the pose and breathe.	Lie on floor with knees bent and put knees directly over heels. Place your arms at your side.Exhale, then press feet into floor as you lift hips up. Breathe slowly. Lower your hips down gently and repeat a few times.
7. Sitting Twist & Stretch	8.Meditation/Stillness & Joy
Stretches shoulders, hips and back.	*Centres the mind, body and soul.*
Sit on the floor with your legs crossed, or on a chair. Inhale then exhale as you twist gently around to the right. Hold as you take a few breaths and feel into it. Switch sides and repeat. Move one of your arms above your head and tilt your torso over to your side and feel the stretch. Do on other side. Repeat mindfully several times.	Sit or lie down. Close your eyes, if you wish and breathe. Take your attention to the flow of air that comes in and out of your body. Relax and breathe deeply. Open your heart and feel your emotions. If you wish, allow joy, happiness and peace to flow through your body. Be aware of how your body feels when positive emotions flow through it.

CHAPTER 17

Ethics, Clients & How We Tick

Code of Ethics

Ethics are important to have so that you respect others and uphold a good reputation.

Ethical codes to consider:

- Only advertise what you have training, expertise, experience and qualifications in.

- Do not diagnose an illness or health problems unless you have the qualifications to do so.

- Do not put down other therapists.

- Keep sessions confidential. Respect your client's privacy.

- If you write written notes make sure they are stored in a safe, secure place.

- Have empathy and understand that clients may be dealing with sensitive issues that may make them anxious and uptight.

- Be polite and considerate towards your clients.

- Be aware of your client's personal belief systems such as their religious beliefs.

- Do not touch a client without their permission.

- Children: Check with your insurance company as some places say that children 16 years or under cannot attend a session without a parent/guardian present or permission in writing.

"Intuition is an art, not a science."[59]

How to Read & Heal Professionally with Clients

Psychic information is only a guide and if you wish to change the outcome you can by adjusting your thoughts, intentions and actions. All that comes to us is for our highest good. Even our challenges can become our greatest gifts as we receive so much knowledge, wisdom and insight from them.

In any kind of healing and psychic development, one must be considerate of the client's feelings. Saying negative or traumatising comments to a client can really pull some people downward into a negative spiral and highly anxious state. I also remind students that the spirit world is very cryptic and that we need to be careful about how we interpret the messages.

I respect and honour that other people work differently to me and that's okay. We all have our own way of approaching life and our work. But working with clients is a heart affair. It's a real privilege and honour to sit in front of another human being and listen to their heart. We must treat this exchange with respect and consideration.

Be aware of your time frame. Also, if you have a day of clients make sure to schedule in breaks so you can have a healthy snack and

---

59 Dale. C. (2013) *The Subtle Body Practise Manual* (p.88), Sounds True, CO.

rest. Taking breaks and respecting your own energy levels will help to ensure you do not burn out.

It's good to wash your hands in-between clients especially after hands-on healing to refresh the energy. Sometimes I spray some essential oils on my hands too.

After seeing clients I ask the universe to protect and guide them. This ritual helps me to release my clients with love and good wishes.

Phone Psychic work

I worked for almost 2 years as a psychic phone reader. It was a very interesting experience. I used to do five-hour shifts and it was convenient to work from home.

I learnt some amazing things while being a psychic on the phone lines. Firstly it helped me to really tune into my own psychic senses as I only had the sound of someone's voice to connect with. There are some brilliant psychics who work on phone lines. Like all professions, some of the psychics on some phone lines are not as skilled as others.

I remember many years ago being on the other end of the phone line myself. I remember calling psychic lines to help me in my personal life. I found different psychics gave me different viewpoints yet it was helpful to have someone to chat with. Most of them were caring and kind which helped me get through some distressing times in my life. Never did I think that years later I would be doing the same thing!

Pearls of Wisdom

The universe delivers everything we need on a platter. The universe communicates to us through songs, media, words, a person or a feeling. Take notice of the signs around you. If you are unsure of which step to take, ask for help and guidance. Know that in a few days you'll receive a sign about which path is right for you.

Sometimes I'm driving along, thinking about a direction to take, and the number plate of the car in front of me has a number plate with the letters YES on it. That's a very clear answer from the universe! Triple numbers such as 111, 222, 333 and so on are signs the spirit world is around you and is supporting you on your journey. The other day I saw the numbers 123 which means everything is in perfect order.

Sometimes a bird will squawk really loudly near me. I tune into its energy and ask it for a message. One day I was awoken by two black crows loudly sqawking to each other outside my home. My alarm was set for a later time but I realised the birds were there to wake me up earlier. Rising earlier meant I could fit in extra jobs which helped my day run more smoothly. I feel the universe was supporting me and sending the birds to help my day flow better.

I love being aware of the signs spirit gives me. They are always there to help and assist us. I love asking them for help and seeing the support that follows. The spirit world is a divine energy that connects with us through tingles, energetic hugs, animal signs and numbers. Recently a client left my reading room and, as we were saying goodbye a large magnificent butterfly circled his head. His mother had just come through our session and he felt the butterfly was a sign from her. Magic is real and it exists all around us. The earthly physical plane we live in can sometimes be challenging and but rising above the negativity allows us to see the beauty, the grace and the marvellous opportunity this plane offers us. Living on this planet allows us to learn how to love, to give and to receive. Everything is an opportunity to grow, to heal and to discover who we truly are. How fortunate we are to have this earth plane to be our classroom for learning, making mistakes and achieving our goals!

Emotions and Themes

The University of Glasgow, in 2014,[60] stated that there are four basic emotions: happy, sad, afraid, and angry. Its important we feel and experience all these emotions and let them speak to us.

Our body is a reflection of our subconscious. If we become aware of what our body is doing then we can tap into what feelings, and emotions, are locked away deep inside us. Feelings and emotions need expression and they want to be heard. We get healthy and well when we listen to our heart, mind and body. Every physical problem stems from an emotional problem. It's a joy to be able to go deep within to find the root cause of our issues.

The tables below highlight the way our beliefs and theories impact our lives. What theories and beliefs run through your life? Where do they stem from? You may wish to write down your answers so you can tap into the energy better.

Table 17.1

Beliefs	Feelings (Linked to those Beliefs)
I am not good	Unhappy
I am not worthy	Sad
I am unlovable	Angry
I am powerless	Afraid

Table 17.2

Themes to Heal	Themes we Desire
Betrayal	Support
Humiliation/Shame	Justice
Abandonment	Safety
Neglect	Presence
Rejection	Love

---

60 http://www.theatlantic.com/health/archive/2014/02/new-research-says-there-are-only-four-emotions/283560/

"Life travels in a spiral, not a straight line. As we cycle and recycle through our past, we can see what is of use to us and we can discard the rest."[61]

The Spiral of Life

Life themes of Betrayal, Humiliation/Shame, Abandonment, Neglect and Rejection spiral around and through us. This spiral pattern goes around our body and connects through every chakra, or gland, from our base chakra up to our crown chakra.

Every time the spiral ascends up our body it goes into each chakra centre and gives us an opportunity to clear and heal the themes. Our soul chooses to encounter certain themes (or patterns) in a lifetime. Sometimes our themes re-occur so we have to revisit those emotions and patterns.

Each time the themes come into our life we address them at the chakra they are at. We have the opportunity to heal the theme at a chakra. The next time the theme will appear at a higher up chakra for another soul lesson to be experienced. When each chakra clears the themes (patterns and emotions) then the cycle will end.

Sandy was feeling abandoned by her Mum and she also felt abandoned in her relationships. We regressed her back to where the theme of abandonment began and it surfaced in her childhood when she was abused.

Sandy had more understanding now about why abandonment issues existed in her life. Sandy decided to alter her mindset and change some of the behaviours that were keeping her stuck in the same theme. Sandy also realised that she was abandoning herself by not looking after her needs properly.

---

61 Wolf, L. (2009) *Shamanic Breathwork* (p.212) Bear & Company, Vermont.

With more self-care and self-nurturing Sandy decided to devote time to healing her inner self. Over time Sandy was more aware of her patterns and began to make new decisions and new choices that helped to embrace a healthier way of living and loving.

Restriction Theme

Alyssa came to see me for a psychic reading. She had been to many psychics and had a healthy scepticism about them. Alyssa sat in front of me with a cynical look on her face. Straight away I tuned into Alyssa's aura and her guide showed me an image of two wrists being tied together.

I thought this was an odd image so I asked the guide, telepathically, for more information. I sensed that this client's theme in life was about restriction. I shared this information with Alyssa and she sternly told me that she didn't agree.

I continued to press on, giving pertinent information through reading tarot and doing palmistry. Alyssa finally admitted that an issue in her life was bothering her.

"So, you're feeling restricted then?" I remarked. She grumpily said "Oh, I suppose so."

Spirit always come through to help with getting a message across, even if someone resists the message at the time!

The Theatre of Life

Imagine this, at the Theatre of Life there is a stage. There's an actor, a director and a producer. There are also other actors who are part of this magical play at the theatre.

Imagine that you are the actor, but you haven't seen the script. You are just going on gut feeling and intuition. The director is guiding you. You have to listen carefully and be aware of what the director wants you to do next in this play. The director also gives you choice and free will to create your own drama but at other times he guides you on what to do next.

Life is a bit like that. It seems like it's a theatrical play but there's no script. You have control over some of what you do in life, but at other times things seem destined for you. Flow, trust, be intuitive and work with the director (universe) to create a script (life path) that is effective, meaningful and purposeful for you.

When the script seems to put you in a challenging role know that it soon will pass and that you can write and create your way out of that "scene."

What sort of life are you designing for yourself? Are you working with the universe to create a meaningful script, using your skills, talents, abilities and know-how? Or, are you wasting your Soul's energy by depleting it with useless thoughts, foods, actions and habits?

Karma Decoy

We don't just work on our own personal karma, sometimes we are here to help others sort out their issues and beliefs from past lives and past experiences. Have you ever not meant to hurt someone but they have taken something the wrong way and they're upset? You are being used by the universe, as a trigger, to help that person identify their blocks and challenges, which they may be avoiding. It's best to support the person but to also highlight that it was unintentional. The trigger was activated to help the person release pent-up blocks in their soul and emotions.

Gratitude Breeds Gratitude

Thank the universe for what you have thus far. I know when someone thanks me for something it makes me feel appreciated and I am more likely to want to do more for that person. The universe is just the same. If it feels you are grateful for what you have, then it will give you more. Does the universe know your heart is open and ready to receive more in life?

Your Choices

> *"The self you are today will also give way to a newer self. Much like a snake that sheds its skin, or the caterpillar that becomes a butterfly, you will continue to evolve over time."*[62]

I love the way caterpillars are transformed into butterflies. We all have the ability to fly and shine.

A pearl forms when an irritant, such as a food particle, becomes trapped in the mollusk. The oyster protects itself from the intruder with a layer of crystals. This then creates a pearl. So if we send love

---

62 Wolf, L. (2009) *Shamanic Breathwork* (p.216) Bear & Company, Vermont.

and healing to the people who annoy and irritate us we can create gems too!

I am constantly amazed at the grace and love this Universe has. At times things seem turbulent and upsetting but in the darkest moments it is wise to take time to reflect and to see the gift in the shadows. Sometimes it's hard to see the jewel, but in time it will be revealed. What choices are you going to make to create an outcome that is healing for all concerned? Are you going to get on the same bandwagon as everyone else and whinge and complain, or are you going to walk to the beat of a different drum and rise above it all?

Sometimes we need people who are going to make a difference. Who think outside the box. People who know that we all attract to us what we need in life.

Sometimes we need to be real, genuine and honest about what we feel. Delivering what we need to say from our heart with love will come across differently than if we share something from ego or revenge-type behaviour. Everyone on this planet is a part of the whole. You can make a difference, not just to your life, but to the world with your positive actions and attitudes.

Exercise: Transforming Relationships

I used this exercise with a challenging co-worker and I was amazed at the results.

1. See the person in your mind's eye.
2. Visualise a relaxing garden/ocean setting. See both of you in the garden.
3. Tune into how you both feel. Intuitively speak the words you need to say to this person.
4. Thank them for the lesson and for their spirit. Honour them and send them love.

5. Visualise the future and see yourself and this person smiling at each other. Send love, kindness and peace to yourself and the other person. Feel good in knowing that as humans we all make mistakes, errors and poor judgement, but we all have the power to improve, shine and redeem ourselves!

Part 3
Our Divine Universe

CHAPTER 18

Psychic Science & Quantum Physics

It's important to understand that there is a link between science and spirituality. Learning about both will help you to have a great respect for this world and your place in it.

Brain and Heart Power

We connect to people around us in mysterious ways but science has proven that the heart is the biggest source of electromagnetic energy in the human body. They found there is an electromagnetic (energetic communication) between people.

"The magnetic field produced by the heart is more than 100 times greater in strength than the field generated by the brain and can be detected up to 3 feet away from the body."[63]

---

63 McCraty, R. (2015) *Science of the heart*, Volume 2. HeartMath Institute, US.

HeartMath research revealed that people, and their pets' heart waves, sync in with each other. Even couples that sleep next to each other tap into each others heart rhythm.

"We have been surprised at the high degree of heart-rhythm synchrony observed in couples while they sleep."[64] The heart's magnetic field extends out into the area around us. This may be why you intuitively pick up on people, and energies, around you.

Our Amazing Brain

Understanding the human brain will help you to understand yourself, your clients and people in general. I know how much it has impacted my life and helped me to handle situations more effectively.

---

64 McCraty, R. (2015) *Science of the heart*, Volume 2. HeartMath Institute, US.

Science has made some new discoveries such as realising the brain can rewire itself. It's called **neuroplasticity**. Neuroplasticity is the ability of your brain to change and adapt to your experiences. Science now knows we can rewire brain circuits and grow new neural pathways, just like a house electrical network can be rewired to work better and run new circuits. So if you want to have a good brain, science has proven that you need enjoyable exercise, fun hobbies, good sleep, low stress levels and good food.

"Old neural patterns are continuously being overwritten by new ones."[65]

Research[66] from the Cochrane Institute in Wales showed that five activities—exercise, not smoking, drinking no more than a glass of wine a day, eating four servings of fruit and vegetables daily and being a normal weight can reduce the risk of developing dementia by an amazing 60 per cent.

Remember too much stress can be harmful to your brain. Studies are showing that when corticosteroid (the stress hormone) was increased that neurogenesis (brain growth) decreased. In fact, chronic stress can shrink the brain, making it hard to learn new information and more of a challenge to remember the information you already have.

As you know, food is paramount to good health and good brain connections. By choosing good food habits we not only have stronger bodies but our moods are happier too as the gut sends up happy chemicals to your brain.

"Your gut is your second brain; gut bacteria transmit information from your GI tract to your brain via your vagus nerve. Just as you have

---

65 http://articles.mercola.com/sites/articles/archive/2015/01/15/neuroplasticity-brain-health.aspx

66 www.abc.net.au/radionational/programs/allinthemind/neuroplasticity-and-how-the-brain-can-heal-itself/6406736

neurons in your brain, you also have neurons in your gut—including neurons that produce neurotransmitters like serotonin, which is linked to mood."[67]

Our Clever Brain

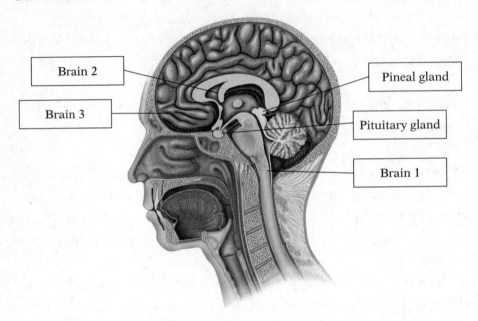

Figure 18.1

Brain 1: This brain controls movement, breathing, circulation, hunger and reproduction. It is territorial.

Brain 2: Is linked to our feelings and emotions. It stores memories like a filing cabinet. It controls our hormones and temperature. Part of limbic system.

Brain 3: This brain is linked to logic, speech and writing. It makes decisions and choices. It processes information from our senses

---

67 http://articles.mercola.com/sites/articles/archive/2015/01/15/neuroplasticity-brain-health.aspx

(touch, sight, facial expressions and tone of voice.) Linked to movement and conscious brain. Helps with intuititve and psychic senses.

Table 18.1

	Name	**Areas**	**Main Function**	**Typical Animal**
Brain 1	Reptilian Brain (unconscious)	Brain stem and cerebellum	Survival instinct. Fight, flight, freeze (run, argue or freeze). Affects our breathing, movement, BP and heartrate. *Am I safe?*	Snakes, crocodiles
Brain 2	Limbic system – Mammalian Brain (subconscious)	Includes amygdala, hippocampus, hypothalamus and thalmus. Affects our temperature, hunger, thirst and sleep and wake cycles.	Feelings and memories. Also affects our endocrine/gland system which is linked to our chakras. Does *not* know difference between reality or imagination. *Am I loved?*	Dogs, cats
Brain 3	Neocortex (conscious)	Cortex	Reasoning, logic, speech, dreams, visions and planning. *What can I learn from this?*	Gorillas, chimpanzees and human beings.

If we visualise negative experiences, we wire them more deeply into our brain.[68] Visualising or remembering pleasant, happy experiences makes the brain think they are real so the circuits in the brain still activate. Brain scans even show that if someone mentally thinks about doing their music practise it registers in the brain nearly the same as if they did the real physical practise.

---

68 Doidge, N. (2015) *The Brains Way of Healing* (p.215) Penguin, NY.

Pineal gland

The Pineal gland is the size of a rice grain, but holds magical qualities. It's called pineal as it looks similar to a pinecone yet it's only 0.8 cm long![69]

The Pineal gland is linked to the 7th chakra and our 3rd eye which is situated in-between our eyebrows.

The Pineal gland makes the melatonin hormone which helps your circadium rhythm, which is our sleep/wake cycle, throughout the day. The pineal also influences our hormones and stress levels.

DMT (Dimethyltryptamine)

DMT is a neurotransmitter that is found in humans, plants and animals. It is said to be a part of us that helps expand to higher consciousness. Some people call DMT the spirit molecule.[70]

DMT is also found in some psychedelic substances.

So far research on rats[71] shows that DMT is also produced naturally in the brain. Humans given DMT report seeing Beings and have other heightened experiences.

When we meditate the DMT in our brain will naturally heighten and therefore we may "see" things. The lungs are also said to produce DMT, although further research is required in this area.[72]

Exercise: Pineal Power

1. Relax and breathe deeply into your lungs, abdomen and right down to your toes. Feel the heavenly oxygen finding its way into every part of your Being. Repeat several times.

---

69 https://www.britannica.com/science/pineal-gland
70 Dale. C. (2013) *The Subtle Boy Practise Manual* (p.192), Sounds True, CO.
71 http://littleatoms.com/science/psychedelic-drug-could-explain-our-belief-life-after-death
72 https://www.sociedelic.com/the-future-of-dmt-research-with-dr-rick-strassman/

2. Call on your own Spiritual essence to come fully into your space and your aura. Connect lovingly with your Higher self. Have the intention of focusing on your beliefs in this meditation.

3. Call in your main spirit guide to support and help you.

4. Connect into your heart chakra in the centre of your chest.

5. Take your focus and awareness into your pineal gland in the mid-part of your head.

6. Imagine going into your pineal gland. The pineal is like a portal, or tunnel of energy, which opens up into another realm where there is love, power and brilliance. Be aware of any colours, sensations and images that may appear to you.

7. Allow yourself to be transported to where you need to go.

8. Allow insight and knowingness to come to you.

9. Beliefs

   State, in present tense, your beliefs, such as – I'm successful at work, I am a loving, kind partner, I am a devoted parent. These beliefs will be more powerful now as you are in a deep, deep state so your subconscious will absorb them better. Note: Be aware of any thoughts and feelings you have when going into a deep sleep as these will influence your subconscious as well.

Electrolytes for Energy

We need electrolytes as they help us have energy. If you are tired, (or are getting twitches, cramps or feeling weak) you may need more electrolytes in your body from foods and fluids. Foods such as fruit and vegetables provide energy to our bodies as they have electrolytes in them. Magnesium is an electrolyte as it transports electrical energy around our body as that's what electrolytes do! Other electrolytes are potassium, sodium, calcium, chloride and hydrogen phosphate. Fruits and vegetables have electrolytes in them such as sodium, potassium, calcium and magnesium.

"An electrolyte is a substance that produces an electrically conducting solution when dissolved in water. Electrolytes carry a charge and are essential for life. All higher forms of life need electrolytes to survive."[73]

As you may know sodium, potassium and magnesium are all minerals in the body. We are made of minerals. They actually burned elements[74] with a flame and discovered that some have colours. Zinc was coloured blue/green; mercury red; sodium yellow, potassium lilac, calcium was an orange colour. I'm not surprised because we are made of colours. Our aura is colourful and I see that around people when I open my third eye to have a look. Crystals are also made of minerals.

Magnesium

Some clients come to me with a shaky tongue or hands and this can be a sign of magnesium deficiency. Cramps can also be a sign of magnesium deficiency as well as sugar cravings. See your health-care professional if you feel you are lacking magnesium and remember too many magnesium supplements in the body can cause loose stools so be aware of this as magnesium is a natural relaxant.

Elements

It is fascinating to understand what we are made of. Did you know your body is made up of just six main elements? These elements are oxygen, carbon, hydrogen, nitrogen, calcium, and phosphorus.[75] The top three elements of the human body are oxygen, carbon and hydrogen. Here's the breakdown for you:

---

73 britannica.com
74 wiki/flame-test
75 Harper, Rodwell & Mayes, *Review of Physiological Chemistry*, 16th ed., Lange Medical Publications, Los Altos, California 1977.

Table 18.2

Oxygen — 65.0%	Potassium — 0.4%
Carbon — 18.5%	Sulfur — 0.3%
Hydrogen — 9.5%	Chlorine — 0.2%
Nitrogen — 3.3%	Sodium — 0.2%
Calcium — 1.5%	Magnesium — 0.1%
Phosphorus — 1.0%	Plus trace amounts of Iodine, Iron and Zinc.

"Carbon is the main component of sugars, proteins, fats, DNA, muscle tissue, pretty much everything in your body."[76] Diamonds are made from carbon like us. Diamonds are formed after experiencing pressure and high temperatures.

Light

Light is made up of wavelengths. Each wavelength is a different colour. The sun's light or even a light from a torch, appears to look like white light yet white light encompasses all the colours of the rainbow. A torch and the sun contain all of the wavelengths![77]

You may notice that when the sun's light rays bounce off clear glass rainbow colours form.

Table 18.3

Colour	Wavelength (nm)
Red	780 – 622
Orange	622 – 597
Yellow	597 – 577
Green	577 – 492
Blue	492 – 455

---

76 http://www.huffingtonpost.com.au/entry/humans-carbon-chemist-molecular-bonds_n_2119037
77 http://sciencelearn.org.nz/Contexts/Light-and-Sight/Science-Ideas-and-Concepts/Colours-of-light

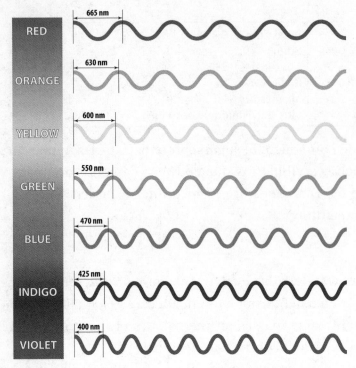

Figure 18.2

Longer wavelengths of light are more of a red colour, while shorter wavelengths of light have more of a blue hue.[78] "Short wavelength photons have a high amount of energy and long wavelength photons less."[79] When you do visualisations, and other work with energy, you can imagine the shorter wavelength colours such as green, blue and violet as these colours have more energy.

Atoms and Molecules

Everything in the universe is made up of atoms and molecules. Molecules consist of atoms which have electrons that spin around and create energy.

---

78 Still, B. *Brain Explains*, (p.62) 2015. Octopus, London.
79 Still, B. *Brain Explains*, (p.62) 2015. Octopus, London.

Did you know that electrons, or energy, can jump from person to person or, thing to thing? Have you ever rubbed a balloon and then put it on a person's hair to see the hair stick out? This is because the electrons have jumped from the balloon over to the hair and caused it to stick up. This can happen when you're doing healings with people. A person's energy, and their electrons, can jump around the room or jump over into your aura.

Quantum Physics

In the last few years I have also became intrigued by Quantum Physics. The wonder and magic of Quantum Physics can help us make sense of the world we live in.

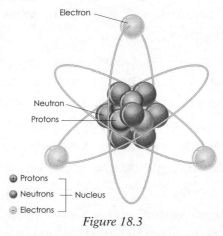

Figure 18.3

Quantum Physics is defined as the study of solids, atoms, molecules, nuclei, particles and light. The world is made up of molecules. These molecules are made up of smaller things called atoms (see picture above of an atom).

E.g. A *water molecule* is made up of atoms –

Atoms (Hydrogen) + Atom (Oxygen).

Albert Einstein said light was really just photons.[80]

---

80 Still, B. (2015) *Brain Explains*, Octopus, London.

Sir Isaac Newton said photons are "little packets of energy."[81] So light = energy. More light means more electrons are released.

When an electron (which is going round an atom) has less energy, it can be detected as there will be less light coming off it. [82] Maybe we humans become tired when we have less energy and hence, less light! When we eat food with light energy from the sun, such as fruit and vegetables, this gives us more energy and vitality.

Did you know that Light is both a wave *and* a particle?

"Light is made up of packets of energy called photons"[83]

Quantum Tunnelling

If you throw a ball against a wall it will bounce back as the atoms in the ball are repelling the electrons in the wall. Yet, Quantum Physics proves that electrons, as wave energy, will pass through a barrier because some electrons have been found on the other side of the barrier! Why? Because the electron acts like a particle when it's in our world but, when it's actually interacting it becomes a wave and, waves CAN go through a barrier, but particles cannot!

"Waves are continuous and do not stop abruptly when they come into contact with a barrier."[84] This makes sense as we know energy (light) can be both a particle and a wave. We know that different levels of energy (light) can act as a particle or a wave so when we heal energy can go into our bodies. I can feel these waves of energy when meditating, exercising, breathing and doing healings. Maybe you feel tingles or vibrations when certain energies are around, or near you. Luckily, science is doing more research in this area.

---

81 Still, B. (2015) *Brain Explains*, (p.44) Octopus, London.
82 Still, B. (2015) *Brain Explains*, Octopus, London.
83 Still, B. (2015) *Brain Explains*, Octopus, London.
84 Still, B. (2015) *Brain Explains*, Octopus, London.

"There are many different types of energy, such as kinetic energy, potential energy, light, sound, and nuclear energy."[85]

We now know electrons can act like waves and this happens in your home each day. Quantum tunnelling exists at home with your electricity. Electrical energy is just the flow of electrons from one area to another. "Metals are good conductors of electricity."[86] It's similar to how water runs through a hose – electrons also run through metal like water down a hose.

Quantum tunnelling is also at play in your computer memory such as USB or RAM. The memory in your computer is made of small boxes that may (or may not) be filled with electrons. [87]

In Quantum physics, quantum bits (in computers) are also called qubits.

MRI machines are called Magnetic Resonance imaging machines because, they can scan the magnetic field of the atoms in your body, and take pictures. Electrons and atoms spin. MRI machines use powerful magnets that take a picture of what's happening, inside our bodies, by getting qubits from the spin of atoms, or electrons in our body.

I love this explanation of what an MRI does to the nucleus of a cell:

"The technique uses a very powerful magnet to align the nuclei of atoms inside the body ... the nuclei produce their own rotating magnetic fields that a scanner detects and uses to create an image."[88]

Atoms

Question: How many atoms in a human body?
Answer: Trillions![89]

---

85 http://chemistry.about.com/od/chemistryglossary/a/energydef.htm
86 Still, B. (2015) *Brain Explains*, Octopus, London.
87 Still, B. (2015) *Brain Explains*, Octopus, London.
88 http://www.livescience.com/39074-what-is-an-mri.html
89 http://chemistry.about.com/od/biochemistry/f/How-Many-Atoms-Are-There-In-A-Human-Cell.htm

Did you know that atoms jiggle around and are measured as a temperature? The higher the temperature the more atoms jiggle! Cooler temperatures mean less jiggles. [90]

When I give Reiki healing to someone they may comment that they feel intense heat in an area of their body. Maybe this means there is more energy going into their body so the atoms jiggle more!

Electrons are smaller than atoms. Electrons have a negative electric charge. Protons have a positive charge and neutrons are neutral. The nucleus is positively charged. Atoms are neutral.[91] Electrons orbit a nucleus just like our moon orbits around planet earth.

"Each atom resembles a solar system."[92]

Atoms have a repeating pattern – just like crytsals do. But some solids, like glass, have an amorphous (no pattern) shape so energy goes through it quicker.[93] Crystals are made up of atoms in a particular structure.

FACT: Humans are classified as subatomic quantum particles!

Static electricity

Static electricity is also another kind of electricity which collects on things such as crystals like Amber. Static electricity occurs if you shuffle your feet along carpet or, rub a balloon on your clothes to make it stick. This is because electrons are more powerfully pulled from one material than the other. This is called an electron swap. The scientific word for it is triboelectricity!

"When we separate the materials, the electrons effectively jump ship to the material that attracts them most strongly. As a result, one

90 Still, B. (2015) *Brain Explains*, Octopus, London.
91 Maneb, E. & Hoehn LC (2106) *Human anatomy & physiology*, Pearson, USA.
92 https://student.societyforscience.org/article/we-are-stardust
93 Green. D. (2010) Chemistry, Kingfisher, London.

of the materials has gained some extra electrons (and becomes negatively charged) while the other material has lost some electrons (and
becomes positively charged)."[94]

I think this electron swap can also happen in humans. Do you sometimes feel different after engaging with another person? Or maybe
you have gone to a shopping centre and felt like you have picked up
some extra energy (electrons)?

Sometimes we need to ground ourselves and place our feet on the
earth so we can swap electrons with the earth. I find it's magical to sit,
walk or lie on the earth. Research shows earthing (i.e. grounding) is
a brilliant way to help one's health by reducing pain, improving sleep
and relaxing us. Get on the earth with your bare feet or, lie on the
grass and allow the earth's vibration to heal you. [95]

Quantum Entanglement

Quantum entanglement is when
2 objects are separated yet they
still have a connection to each
other. Science found out that if
you measure the property of one
member of an entangled pair
then you know the property of
the other! Even Einstein called

quantum entanglement "spooky action at a distance." [96]

It has been shown that people in different rooms can still have an
effect on each other because of quantum entanglement. HeartMath
research shows couples who sleep in the same bed have an effect on
each other so be careful of your mood when you go to sleep! Also
healers have an affect on their clients as their energy will entangle

---

94 http://www.explainthatstuff.com/how-static-electricity-works.html
95 http://www.ncbi.nlm.nih.gov/pmc/articles/PMC3265077/
96 https://www.sciencedaily.com/releases/2014/03/140318140537.htm

with another so it's important that you are centred and call in energies from the cosmos, and the earth, to balance and centre you.

Emotional contagion states that we can take on the mood of those around us. Our **Mirror Neuron System** has neurons (nerves) in the brain that mimic, or copy, people's facial expressions, attitudes and even tone of voice. So be aware of the influence your emotions and body language have on others. You do not need to take on other peoples energies.

Instead be present and honour them by understanding that the challenge, or concern, they have at the moment is happening for a Divine reason. Your aim is to stay balanced and strong for them, not take on the negative energy – this will help them more than if you emotionally (or subconsciously) feel you have to take on their issues.

If you feel you are becoming lost in another person's emotions, or energy, take some deep breaths and tap into your wise self so you can shift the energy in positive ways.

Psychiatrist Dan Siegel[97] explains emotional entanglement as "instead of two separate individuals who can find a reliable connection

97   Siegel, D. (2016) *Mindsight* (p.180), Scribe, Australia.

with each other, they have become entangled." Dan describes emotional entanglement as not seeing someone else as a separate person, for example, if Jodie cancels an appointment, you view this as meaning it was because of how Jodie feels about you rather than she is unable to make the appointment for her own personal reasons.

Take time to differentiate between yourself and another person and know that we all have free will and our own decisions to make. Remember to do your best and allow others to take responsibility for their own actions.

If you are triggered by someone else's energy, or story, seek help or share it with a close friend. Writing (or typing) your emotions and feelings in a journal is very healing. Journal writing helps one to reflect, and process, some of the events that happen in life both professionally and personally. Scientific evidence[98] shows that journal writing helps our immune system and therefore our overall health.

Journalling our feelings also allows us to access our creativity and intuition better so that we can solve issues, feel less stressed and have more clarity about our life.

Exercise: Two Lives Meditation

We can live two lives at once by using our imagination.

Imagine you are in this world now but you also see yourself in another world with everything that you desire in it.

It's almost like having 2 realities at once.

Your brain thinks that what you imagine is real so have fun with imagining that you are here right now but the things around you may look different.

In this other world, your senses are alive: sight, sound, touch, smell, taste.

1. Imagine this other world in your mind's eye overlaying everything.

---

98 http://psychcentral.com/lib/the-health-benefits-of-journaling/

2. Dream of what you desire. Feel it. Ask your Guides to show you if you are sabotaging these wishes on some level.

3. Maybe you are sitting in your office but imagine that you are on a beach, the seagulls are around you, the sun is warm, you feel relaxed and happy and the sounds of the waves make you feel peaceful. The blue colour of the ocean makes you feel tranquil.

4. Try this exercise again, imagining a different scenery, notice what happens to your mind and body as it taps into this new reality.

Notice: Does your breathing change, do your muscles relax more? Do you smile or feel happier?

CHAPTER 19

The Cosmos

"The organs of the human body are the essence of the stars and planets energies."[99]

Understanding the cosmos, and the world we live in, helps us to get a different perspective on our lives and the universe around us. The Universe began about 13.8 billion years ago when the Big Bang occurred.[100] The Big Bang is described as "the cosmic explosion that marked the beginning of the universe."[101]

After the Big Bang two elements existed. These two elements were hydrogen and helium. Other elements came along after nuclear fusion occurred. Nuclear fusion means the joining of atoms. Nuclear fusion needs heat and pressure to work, which apparently, the stars are very good at!

"Nuclear fusion takes place in the heart of stars and causes them to burn."[102]

99   Chia, M. & Chia, M. (1990) *Internal Organs Chi Massage* (p.19), Healing Tao Books, NY.
100 Steven Desch of Arizona State University in Tempe. An astrophysicist,
101 http://www.merriam-webster.com/dictionary/big%20bang
102 http://physics.about.com/od/glossary/g/nuclearfusion.htm

The explosion of a star is called a supernova. This happens when the star has run out of hydrogen. When a supernova occurs, a big cloud of dust and gas appears.

The solar system consists of our sun, planets, meteorites, comets and asteroids. Our solar system lives in the Milky way. The Milky way galaxy is like a spiral band which has trillions of stars in it.

The Milky way loses stars and makes new ones just like our bodies lose cells and makes new ones.[103] The surprising thing is there are other galaxies out there that science does not even know about yet!

"The solar system is believed to be about 4.6 billion years old."[104]

Astrophysicist Dr Paul Francis gave a talk about astronomy one starry night in Canberra. I asked Dr Francis about the Milky way – which contains our whole solar system. I knew that the Milky way moved in a spiral pattern but I wanted to know whether it moved in a clockwise or, anticlockwise way. Dr Francis replied that the Milky way moves in both directions as it depends on which side you're looking at it! I feel the spiral pattern of the Milky way relates to some of the spiral Reiki healing symbols as well as shells, and other things in nature, that have a natural spiral design.

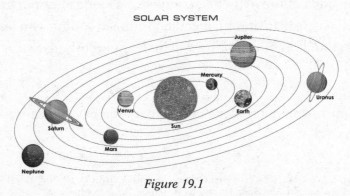

Figure 19.1

103 http://www.universetoday.com/22285/facts-about-the-milky-way/
104 http://curious.astro.cornell.edu/our-solar-system/planets-and-dwarf-planets

Sun

The Sun is the centre of our solar system. It is approximately 150 million kms away from our Earth and is made of gas, so you can't stand on it as it's not solid! It is classed as an average sized star. The sun is 400 times bigger than the moon and is 400 times further away so that makes the sun and moon appear to be the same size.

Inner planets

The planets closest to the sun are called inner planets. They are Mercury, Venus, Earth and Mars. These four planets are also called *terrestrial* planets. These planets are rocky with solid surfaces.

Gas Giants

Next, we have the four gas giants. They are Jupiter, Saturn, Uranus and Neptune. These four outer planets have no solid surface as they are made of hydrogen and helium. Jupiter, Saturn, Uranus and Neptune are also called *jovian* or *jupiterlike*.

Mercury

Mercury is the closest planet to the sun. It has a rocky surface and many craters are found on it. Mercury also has mountains and valleys. Mercury is the smallest of all our planets. It has more iron in it than other planets. Mercury was named after a Roman messenger God. [105]

Venus

Venus is the hottest planet in our solar system.[106] It's too hot for space-craft to land on it. Venus has volcanoes on it and is a similar size to earth, but no water has been found on it. Venus was named after the Roman goddess of love and beauty.

---

105 http://www.universetoday.com/
106 http://www.universetoday.com/

Moon

The Earth's moon takes approximately 29 days to go around the earth. The moon is mainly made of rock and there's no water on it. The moon has an iron rich core.

The moon's surface has many craters. These craters were caused by asteroids hitting it. Did you know that when it's a full moon the moon's brightness comes from the sun's rays? The moon just reflects the light of the sun. In 1969 Neil Armstrong walked on the moon.

Mars

Mars has valleys and canyons on it. It's half as wide as the earth. The temperature varies quite a bit. Mars has two moons which are called Phobos and Deimos which were named after mythological characters. Mars is named after the Roman god of wars.[107] Mars is known as the red planet due to its red colour. The red/orange colour is because of the iron oxide (hematite) it contains. The soil on Mars contains elements of magnesium, sodium, potassium and chlorine. [108]

Jupiter

Jupiter is the largest of all the planets. Jupiter is a gas planet so it has no solid surface for spacecraft to land on. Jupiter has very cold temperatures. Did you know that 1300 earths could fit inside Jupiter![109] Jupiter has a red spot (storm) on it that scientists say is slowly decreasing in size. In 1979 they discovered that Jupiter's rings were made of dust. Jupiter's atmosphere is approximately 90% Hydrogen and 10% helium. It has 67 moons which is the most of any planet in our solar system.[110] The word Jupiter comes from the king of the Roman gods.

---

107 Dickmann, N. (2015) The Solar System, QEB,US.
108 http://www.universetoday.com/
109 http://www.nasa.gov/audience/forstudents/k-4/stories/nasa-knows/what-is-jupiter-k4.html
110 http://www.universetoday.com/

Saturn

Saturn has 62 moons of which Titan is the largest moon. Saturn's nine rings are made of dust, rock and ice. It's the second biggest planet. It's a cool planet although it can vary. Saturn is made mostly of hydrogen and helium. Named after the Roman god of agriculture. Saturn has a golden hue which is said to come from ammonia ice crystals.

Uranus

Uranus's colour is blue/green and it is one of the coldest planets. In 1977 it was found that Uranus has 13 rings. It also has 27 moons. It is twice as far from the sun as Saturn is, so there is a huge gap between Saturn and Uranus. Uranus was discovered in 1781 by William Herschel, via his telescope.[111] Uranus was named after the Greek god of the sky. It has hydrogen and helium in its atmosphere. Uranus can be seen with the naked eye.[112]

Neptune

Neptune is blue in colour and is the Roman god of the sea. It consists of rocks, ice and gas. It is a cold and stormy planet. There is also no solid surface on Neptune. Neptune is four times larger than the Earth and is our solar system's 4th largest planet. It has 5 thin dust rings and 13 moons. Its largest moon is called Triton.[113] Neptune's atmosphere is 80% hydrogen and 19% helium. Neptune cannot be seen with the naked eye.[114]

Pluto

Pluto was discovered in 1930. In 2006 it was classed as a dwarf planet. Did you know an 11-year-old English girl, named this planet?[115]

111 Dakota, H. (2008) Space, Scholastic, NY.
112 http://www.universetoday.com/
113 Dickmann, N. The Solar System, 2015. QEB, US.
114 http://www.universetoday.com/
115 http://www.universetoday.com/

Pluto is so cold that the atmosphere freezes. The top surface is made of frozen nitrogen. Pluto has a rocky core and also has mountains on it. Pluto has 5 moons. The largest moon is called Charon.[116] NASA says Pluto has a love-heart shape pattern on its surface.[117]

Dwarf Planets

Ceres, in 2006, went from being classed as an asteroid to a dwarf planet. Eris, Makemake and Haumea, are also dwarf planets.

Comets

Comets are made of ice and dust. Comets grow tails when they get near the sun as the heat affects the ice. Gas may form which can be seen to look like a blue tail. Comets also have long dust tails.

Asteroids

Asteroids are small rocky objects in our Solar System. Most asteroids orbit around the sun between Mars and Jupiter. This area, between Mars and Jupiter, is called the Asteroid Belt. Vesta is a rocky asteroid.

"We think that the total mass of all the asteroids combined is less than that of the Moon."[118]

Meteors

Meteors are also called shooting stars. Meteors may appear like short, white streams across the sky. Meteors occur because small pieces of dust burn up.

---

116 http://www.universetoday.com/
117 http://www.universetoday.com/
118 http://curious.astro.cornell.edu/our-solar-system/planets-and-dwarf-planets

Chiron

Chiron is classed as an asteroid and a comet.[119] In ancient mythology Chiron is the wise healer who has the upper body of a human and lower body of a horse. Chiron was discovered in 1977. Chiron is located between the planets Saturn and Uranus. [120]

Table 19.1

Planet	Distance to the SUN (km)	Orbits around the SUN in...	Diameter across (km)
Mercury	58 million	88 days	4878 km
Venus	108 million	225 days	12104 km
Earth	150 million	365.2 days	12756 km
Mars	228 million	687 days	6794 km
Jupiter	778 million	12 years	142800 km
Saturn	1427 million	29.5 years	120000 km
Uranus	2870 million	84 years	51800 km
Neptune	4497 million	164 years	49500 km
Pluto (dwarf planet)	5870 million	248 years	2400 km

This grid highlights how amazing our planets are in distance, size and orbits![121]

Sun's Orbit

I was fascinated to learn that the Sun moves about 70,000 km each hour![122] It takes the sun 225 million years to complete one orbit around the solar system. The planets and asteroids, orbit around the sun so they are also moving with the sun. The diameter of the sun is 109 times bigger than the Earth's diameter.

119 https://astronomynow.com/2015/03/17/chiron-may-be-second-minor-planet-to-possess-saturn-like-rings/
120 http://www.astro.com/astrology/in_wounding_e.htm
121 http://www.slideshare.net/cjordison/astrophysics-part-1-2012
122 https://astrosociety.org/edu/publications/tnl/71/howfast.html

The Earth is moving around the sun at about 30 kilometres per second! So the earth moves approximately 108,000 kilometres per hour.

Stars

There are billions of stars in the galaxy around us. It is said that stars are made of similar elements like the rest of the Universe. Stars are made mainly of hydrogen with small amounts of helium. 73% hydrogen, 25% helium, and the last 2% includes all other elements.[123]

"On a basic quantum level, all the matter in the universe is essentially made up of stardust." [124]

Astrophysicist Karel Schrijver, and his wife, professor Iris Schrijver, believe that our bodies contain cosmic energy from the universe.

"Everything we are and everything in the universe and on Earth originated from stardust, and it continually floats through us even today ... rebuilding our bodies over and over in our lifetimes." [125]

"So most of the material that we're made of comes out of dying stars, or stars that died in explosions. And those stellar explosions continue," suggests Karel Schrijver. [126]

123 http://www.universetoday.com/24796/what-are-stars-made-of/
124 http://www.livescience.com/32828-humans-really-made-stars.html
125 http://news.nationalgeographic.com/2015/01/150128-big-bang-universe-supernova-astrophysics-health-space-ngbooktalk/
126 http://news.nationalgeographic.com/2015/01/150128-big-bang-universe-supernova-astrophysics-health-space-ngbooktalk/

Brightest Stars in the Earth's Sky

One of the brightest stars in our Earth's sky is Sirius. Sirius is also called the Dog Star.[127] Sirius is about twice the size of the sun and 25 times brighter![128] Canopus is another very bright star in our solar system.

Large Stars

Large stars include UY Scuti and VY Canis Majoris. UY Scuti is approximately 30 times bigger than the sun.[129] VY Canis Majoris is "around 270,000 times brighter than the Sun."[130]

Exercise: Cosmic Connection

1. Relax your body and breathe deeply. Bring your attention to focus on a flickering candle or a star in the night sky. (If you are unable to view a real candle or star then you may like to imagine them in your mind's eye.)

2. Continue to relax and breathe as you merge with the essence, and energy, of the candle or star.

3. Open up your heart and smile into your heart area and body.

4. Feel your body deeply connect to the crystals in the earth. Allow your natural intuition and insight to come forward.

5. Communing with the stars is magical. You will telepathically connect to their energies. Tune into their essence. Ask questions and hear the answers that come forth for you. Your guides and higher self are there to help assist you on this earth plane. They so dearly love and appreciate everything you do.

---

127 http://space.about.com/od/stars/tp/brighteststars.htm
128 http://forcetoknow.com/space/top-10-largest-stars-universe.html
129 http://earthsky.org/space/how-big-is-the-biggest-monster-star
130 http://forcetoknow.com/space/top-10-largest-stars-universe.html

6. Now repeat this exercise but this time call in the energy of a planet or planets. You may like to collectively call them all in or, you may sense a certain planet is linking with your energy field. Telepathically connect to its energy. Tune into its essence. Ask questions and hear the answers that come forth for you.

7. Go within to the wisdom in your heart. Feel its energy and vibration. Tell your heart your wishes and goals knowing that your heart loves to see you vibrant, happy and healthy.

YOU Are So Deeply LOVED

Final Note:

I hope that this book brings you greater understanding and knowledge.
May you be filled with passion, purpose and hope!
I wish you much success, peace and joy.
Know that you are greatly loved by a Universe that is magical, powerful and healing.

Love to You,
Anna

Acknowledgements

Thank you to Quantum Physics for showing me that this universe is an incredible place and that we can expect the unexpected because the universe works in magical and mysterious ways!

Thanks to the wonderful family I have. To my parents, Noel and Maria, who are always happy to listen and to love. My gorgeous sister Mary and wise brothers David, Paul, Shane and Nathan and their families, who allow me to test ideas out on them and, for encouraging me along my path.

To my daughter Kira who is kind, smart and loving. To Reecey for his patience and devotion. To my beloved Billy who walks beside me and who loves exploring all things magical with me. To Isaac and Jordan for being real and showing that strength is within all of us.

I am very grateful to the Rockpool Publishing team who gave birth to this book, as a self-published version, and then offered me a publishing contract. Miracles DO happen!

Anna x

"It is impossible to feel unhappy and grateful at the same time- so count your blessings each day and be happy."[131]
Twylah Nitsch

---

131 Wolf, L. (2009) *Shamanic Breathwork* (p.215) Bear & Company, Vermont.

About the Author

Anna Comerford is an award-winning Psychic Medium. Anna was awarded the Australian Psychic of the Year in 2017.

Anna is a Psychic Medium and spiritual teacher who sees Auras and Spirits. She uses Tarot, Numerology, Palmistry and Spirit Guides to give readings and healings that are meaningful & powerful. Anna has seen thousands of clients in her clinic in Canberra, Australia.

Anna has Bachelor degrees in Education and Health Science. She works as a Hypnotherapist, Naturopath, Reiki Master, Psychic Medium, Crystal Healer, Yoga Teacher, Neuropsychotherapist, Coach and Intuitive Astrologer.

Anna runs the School of Higher Learning and teaches courses on Reiki, Healing, Crystals, Abundance, Relationships, Palmistry, Psychic Development, Mediumship and Channelling. Anna enjoys teaching and coaching others to get more meaning, purpose and joy from their life!

Anna has been a qualified schoolteacher for over 30 years. Anna attends fairs and expos where she does readings, talks and workshops. Anna has worked as an international phone psychic. She also does phone/Skype sessions.

Please see annacomerford.com for more details.